MARTHA AND MARY

ANASTASIO BALLESTRERO

MARTHA AND MARY

Meeting Christ as Friend

ST PAULS

Original title: *Marta e Maria. La casa dell'amicizia*
© Figlie di San Paolo, Milano (Italy), 1991

Translated by D. Mary Groves OSB
Cover photograph and graphics by Mary Lou Winters

ST PAULS
Middlegreen, Slough SL3 6BT, United Kingdom
Moyglare Road, Maynooth, Co. Kildare, Ireland

English translation © ST PAULS (UK) 1994

ISBN 085439 483 4

Typeset by TuKan, High Wycombe
Printed by The Guernsey Press Co., Guernsey, C.I.

ST PAULS is an activity of the priests and brothers of the Society of St Paul who proclaim the Gospel through the media of social communication

Contents

II. THE HOUSE OF FRIENDSHIP

Preface

The picture Luke has sketched in chapter 10 at verses 38-42 provides the plan for a series of meditations given in this book.

Jesus, Martha and Mary meet. It is only a meeting. But in a few masterly strokes Luke brings out the sense, the primary meaning. Jesus "entered a certain village, where a woman named Martha welcomed him into her home." Jesus was travelling around. Not by chance, he entered a certain village. A village he knew. And in particular he knew friends living there. So the house he went into belonged to friends. It is as though there is a standing invitation to come in and share. An invitation from whom? and why? "She had a sister named Mary, who sat at the Lord's feet and listened to what he was saying." Whether intuitively, or by reasoning, or through faith, we do not know how it was, Mary has perceived the deep meaning of friendship with Jesus. Their attitudes and gestures, of Jesus as well as of Mary, express all its pregnant meaning. These and other features have a reference to words spoken by Jesus elsewhere: "I have called you friends, because I have made known to you everything that I have heard from my Father" (Jn 15:15b). His words are no empty unattached phrases but expressions of life. They show us how to cope with life, lead us by way of faith and hope to what is of true value. A contemporary writer, Kahlil Gibran, says about friendship: "There should be no other intention in friendship than a mutual spiritual discovery. For love which does not seek only to disclose one's mystery is not love.... The better part must be for your friend." Words of a poet, which convey the sincere search for the truth of existence.

"Martha was distracted by her many tasks; so she came to him and asked: 'Lord, do you not care that my sister has left me to do all the work by myself? Tell her then to help me.' But the Lord answered her, 'Martha, Martha, you are worried and distracted by many things; there is need of only one thing. Mary has chosen the better part, which will not be taken from her.'" The better part. Mary has chosen to receive the Lord: himself, his words. The better part, which in Gospel terms means: "If you abide in me, and my words abide in you, ask for whatever you wish, and it will be done for you. My Father is glorified by this, that you bear much fruit and become my disciples" (Jn 15:7). In straightforward language the following pages urge us on to search out new aspects of the Christian mystery, to live our encounter with Christ in a new way.

***

Now as they went on their way, he entered a certain village; where a woman named Martha welcomed him into her home. She had a sister named Mary, who sat at the Lord's feet and listened to what he was saying. But Martha was distracted by her many tasks; so she came to him and asked, "Lord, do you not care that my sister has left me to do all the work by myself? Tell her then to help me." But the Lord answered her, "Martha, Martha, you are worried and distracted by many things; there is need of only one thing. Mary has chosen the better part, which will not be taken away from her.

Luke 10:38-42

Introduction

Sought by Christ

When we read the Gospel we can see how the Lord is ever on the move: he journeys, travels the roads, goes out looking for people. This Jesus goes searching, goes out sowing the seed, but his going around, going out to meet others, seems to me deeply expressive of a spiritual reality to which we ought to give more attention. Why?

Because this Lord who comes, journeys, seeks, meets, is a mystery that is continually renewed in our life. It is much truer to say that the Lord seeks us than that we seek him.

And this is not only at the times when we are busy, distracted, preoccupied, overworked, agitated, as so often happens, but it is also true of our times of recollection when we think we are making an intense and thorough-going effort to seek the Lord.

Letting ourselves be sought

This conviction should suggest our approach: to let ourselves be sought by the Lord. Not to set ourselves to find the way to him, to understand his will, to study his mystery, but to let ourselves be sought.

It is also a valuable approach because, especially as things are today, this putting ourselves in a creaturely state of mind and letting ourselves be sought and found, gives inner tranquillity. It quietens down all that turmoil and agitation that afflicts us.

This is an availability that the Lord is asking: to let ourselves be found. Our attitude should be one of acceptance of the one who speaks, who comes to us, who knows what should be done. Let us ask ourselves before the Lord, do we let ourselves be sought or do we shy away, take off, because we have other interests than his glory and his love?

These attitudes of availability and submission seem to me basic.

"Speak, Lord." When we once say that to the Lord, say it twice, a hundred times, we shall find ourselves in an atmosphere of greater spiritual calm, greater interior silence and above all greater freedom.

That is, we shall be free of our usual agitations, our habitual anxieties and disquiet along with the rhythm of life in our day.

By doing this we shall realise a great and fundamental truth: we are created by God. And if that is so, what is there more important to think about than the Lord?

Well then, thinking about the Lord should become something felt deep within us which makes us stand continually in the presence of God.

"The Lord lives, in whose presence I stand", said the prophet Elisha. That sense of the presence of God, that conviction that we are in God, that in God we live, is no easy matter and yet it is the foundation of all.

To be in the presence of God, then, means precisely putting ourselves in God's presence, being conscious that God is present to us and that his presence should rightly remain the most important thing in our life.

The presence of God.

To live 'as if' we were always in God's presence. Well then, why can't we?

It is no fiction that we are always in God's presence: an unfathomable mystery, but the truth. It is no use running away so as not to be in the presence of God. God's presence is unavoidable, mysterious but penetrating in the extreme.

The sense of the presence of God so much needs to be developed in our life. It is possible to advance ceaselessly in this sense of God's presence until, in eternity, we shall in his presence be blessed and fulfilled.

You see how the perception of God's presence is particularly required of us.

Our first duty is that of prayer: a tranquil, varied exercise of prayer, which is an exercise of the presence of God.

Another valuable disposition for bringing out the sense of the presence of God in us is silence: I so much want to recommend it to you. We need to detoxify ourselves from the invasion of words, images, manifold interests. Silence is not a virtue to be practised as a penance. It should become something desired, because when we are silent God speaks. Silence is pregnant with God's presence, quickened by God's voice, the space where we can see, feel, enjoy the Lord.

A third approach could be to put a brake on our restless memory. We live in an age when the human faculty most under pressure and most disturbed is the memory. Once upon a time it could be used to forget, today it has to hoard everything, record everything. I beg you to keep your heart alert, your mind awake, to listen to the Lord, to remain in his presence, but let your memory go.

These are small ways which help to remind us how much we need to make the atmosphere of our spiritual life less heavy, less clouded, less conditioned by an infinity of words, ideas, curiosities, pleasures, which tend to weaken and imprison the soul and weary mind and heart.

Mary, most blessed among all, never allowed herself to be distracted from God's presence. I commend you to her for her to teach you how to live in the presence of God, share with you her compassion. So we will come to see what the Lord is saying to us.

Speak, Lord, for we are listening.

I
THE GUEST

"Today I must come to your house"

The one who is to come

Meditating on Christ's mystery we cannot but notice how along the centuries the Messiah is surrounded with an atmosphere of expectancy: he is the one who is to come and his coming is firmly fixed in the mind of the patriarchs and the pronouncements of the prophets. That is what they call him: the One who is to come.

And the nearer the ages of history approach the time of his coming the more he becomes dominant: "Are you the one who is to come?" (Mt 11:3). The question put by John the Baptist expresses a whole accumulation of desires, expectations, hopes. "Are you the one who is to come?"

The Lord has come, and here we have a mysterious contradiction. While the ardent desire of his coming swells from generation to generation, when he comes he is not accepted.

This is the mystery. They await him and do not accept him; they expect him, know he is to come, and meet him with resistance and rejection. But who are they who do not accept him? St John (1:11) makes a tremendous statement: "his own" did not want to receive him, his own people. This is a mystery we should often meditate, because to welcome the Lord who comes is in truth the greatest responsibility of the human race, our responsibility.

His own did not accept him

Why this mysterious contradiction between expectation of the Lord and his rejection? Because the image of the one who is to come has two very contrasting profiles: he is the one the patriarchs hoped for, the prophets announced, the evangelists revealed; and he is also one who does not match up to the plan put forward by God, the revelation of the Son of the Father, and the rejection which he receives is rejection by the human race which is not looking for a Saviour, but rather prefers its own plans, caprices, vanity and pride.

This contradiction is evinced in the Gospel at every opposition to the Lord. They await the Messiah but they are expecting a man of power who will revive all the proud hopes of a chosen people who have ended by having God for their servant instead of being the servants of God. And then we can understand how it is that only the humble, the simple, the poor acclaim this Lord who comes, while the powerful, the learned, the rich oppose him. Thus the story of the Incarnate Word has the development it has and the ending we all know: the cross.

Characteristic of all the personal vicissitudes of the one who is to come and has come, emerges the fact that Jesus has come to save what was lost, has come to redeem, to restore the dignity of sons and daughters to those who welcome and accept him.

I am saying all this to remind ourselves that the Lord is the saviour of sinners, he is the redeemer of the lost, and that therefore his coming must result in our conversion.

The Lord comes to convert us. He comes to present to us the great grace of making us realise our poverty, our misery, our sins, our laziness and pride, our egoism, our vanity.

The Lord seeks us

I like to picture the Lord coming one day to look for us. We go towards him in our fashion, one which is very like that of Zacchaeus (Lk 19:1-10).

He is a little man but he wants to see Jesus. He climbs up a tree and starts looking, not knowing that the Lord is looking at him as he passes. This is the way with Jesus: Nathanael too he saw when he was under the fig-tree (Jn 1:48). He is a seeker of men and women, of poor people, small of stature and of mind. To these he turns his gaze and with that look decides a life: "Zacchaeus, come down because today I must come to your house." He not only sees him, looks at him, but invites himself to his house, and everyone is shocked because this rogue Zacchaeus is well known for a tax collector and a sinner.

"Today I must come to your house": and what is he going to do in Zacchaeus' house? Zacchaeus makes a feast for him, prepares a banquet, proud perhaps at having the famous Teacher as a guest, but Jesus is entering another house, the house of his conscience and his heart. While the people round are shocked that he should sit at the table of a sinner, Zacchaeus makes profession of his conversion and does so concretely in his life: he has robbed and he will restore; he has profited by others' misfortune and he will make reparation.

From sinners to sons

It is a life turned upside down that the Gospel here announces and proclaims. Zacchaeus has received the Lord into his house, has let him enter, welcomed him by lavishing exterior courtesies upon him, but at the same time has let himself be conquered inwardly: he has heard, has understood, has given himself.

This entering of Jesus into a sinner's life is repeated an infinite number of times in the history of salvation, in so many ways, so many forms, some outspoken, some silent and hidden. One thing is certain: anyone who gives a welcome to the Lord is graced with the gift of conversion.

And it has to be the same for us too: receiving the Lord who changes our life from within, who humbles us with the consciousness of our own misery and blesses us with the experience of his mercy. And the greater the realisation of our misery, the greater the experience of his mercy.

Called by name

Like Zacchaeus we too would taste this grace of conversion and so we have to convince ourselves of certain important things. The first is that the Lord is looking for us, but not like a flock of lost sheep: he seeks us calling us by name, he seeks us in the realities of our life, just as they are. If we succeed in convincing ourselves of this, if we feel ourselves the recipients of a call by name from Jesus, we shall realise that none but he knows what our name conveys.

We do not know who we are, we are always in search of an identity continually eluding us. Well, we are people the Lord is searching for and calling by name, a name which defines us completely. He knows all our thoughts, he sifts all our desires, discerns all our feelings and knows how to unravel the confusion of our conscience with unalterable sweetness.

In short, he helps us to understand ourselves, persuades us of our poverty, the need we have of him. He moves us by the tenderness with which he treats our feeble nature, which in spite of all the promises rebels and stays rebellious. And coming into our house he frees us from the fear of being known to him and fills us instead with the peace of knowing that he understands us. The instinctive attitude of one trying to hide from God (Gen 3:8) disappears from our life, and that is the sign of our conversion: I do not hide, I know that your voice is my salvation and I know that saved in me is not only what I can see but also what you alone can see.

If we can persuade ourselves that conversion is the gift of Christ our Saviour our life is freed, our spirit gains in transparency and, regaining an inner responsiveness, becomes more capable of perceiving the Lord's visits and to share in the beatitude: Happy the meek, for they shall inherit the earth.

Open the door to Christ

We should allow ourselves to be visited in this way by the Lord, should open the door to him as enthusiastically as Zacchaeus did. It is not necessary to understand. It is only necessary for God to become our wisdom, our understanding, our consciousness and our truth.

That, it seems to me, defines what our attitude should be. We shall do no other than follow this reasoning and abandon ourselves to this Lord who never ceased to come, and the more he comes the more he enters in, transforming our whole life.

I have chosen the story of Zacchaeus because it is easy for us to be somewhat caught up in the presumption of being better Christians than others, disciples with more understanding, servants of the Lord who, all things considered, render him greater service. Let us rid ourselves of all that and put ourselves in the attitude of sinners. This is always true, completely true, and we should be humbled by it, for it is not the result of analysis, of our psychological or moral introspection, but comes from the Lord who invariably brings light wherever he goes, light which is life.

And also let us pray a great deal that we may never find ourselves among those of 'his own' who hinder his coming in some way. Let us not flee from this Lord, withdraw ourselves from his presence. Let us not rebel against his will and put hindrances in the way of our consent when he asks it. Such consent is the sign of our fidelity and the pledge of our continued conversion. That conversion is never something in the remote past but always in the present and also, let it be frankly said, in the future.

In this way we shall know the peace which the Lord gives, and find again the simplicity of the children of God which we so much need in order to bear witness to him as we should.

Times of conversion

We have been considering how the Lord invited himself to the house of the tax collector and he did it with a certain peremptoriness: "I must come to your house today" (Lk 19:5). And in that house, despite the murmuring of many, Jesus was saviour because the tax collector had come to welcome him with a whole series of conversions: from surprise at finding himself the object of this invitation, to haste and excitement at bringing his Lord into his house, and then to letting himself be caught up and carried away in his presence.

Believing in Christ

And what are the stages marking the conversion of this sinful tax collector? The first and most radical is that he believed in Jesus when he found himself overcome by his presence. Jesus had requested his hospitality and so converted him, asking him for something, something very ordinary, quite external and which also cost Zacchaeus little because he had plenty of means.

Zacchaeus was not one of those who showed their

disdain because Jesus went with sinners, as was the case with the Pharisees. When Jesus goes to a Pharisee's house, as his guest, the Pharisee is shocked because an unfortunate woman gives him her perfume and her kisses. But Zacchaeus is pleased that Jesus should have come into his house, he feels privileged, honoured. The Saviour's path of mercy has led to him and Zacchaeus believes in him.

But what did Zacchaeus the tax collector believe? His believing in Jesus went beyond the sentiments aroused in him at having the Lord as his guest, beyond the emotion, beyond enthusiasm and affection. Jesus is Saviour and the tax collector believes this without too many mental processes, without any critical outbursts, and Jesus gives him life. Now there is one more who worships Christ, loves him and starts to follow him. That is the great thing about conversion.

Believing in Jesus properly speaking does not mean believing in him in accordance with some ideological or doctrinal choice. It means having with him a deep, unending living relationship.

Examining our faith

We too are visited by Christ, we too are called to conversion, but that requires believing in him. Paradoxical though it may seem, the question we all have to ask ourselves, and I, a Friar and Bishop, put it to myself first of all, is: do I believe in Jesus?

This question of prime importance in testing conversion we should each put to ourselves.

The answer is not easy because to believe in Jesus does not come naturally, is not a result of our culture, or to be met with in the way of speculation or research or knowledge. In order to believe in Jesus we have to have the gift of faith: believing is not giving but receiving. The experience of faith tells us of an inner certainty not grounded in a multiplicity of arguments but in God's revelation: the Father who manifests himself in the Son and the Son who rejoices to be given to us by the Father.

Do we believe in Jesus? I would certainly hope so. What is there more beautiful, more spontaneous, more delightful, than being touched by this certainty, this revelation, this grace? And yet – and here conversion indeed engages the human dimension, which can also disconcert us – to believe in Jesus means to say overcoming the demands of our pride, our dignity. It means rising above these so-called values, to which we are so often tempted to give more importance than to the Lord himself. Believing in Jesus means renouncing so many demands for his sake and setting ourselves to listen to his words and his responses.

Now we can see that believing in Jesus is not something to be done at a stroke however grand a gesture it may be. It is a gift which Christ, sent by the Father, offers us completely gratuitously and in glorious fulness but we cannot hope to receive it all at once. It becomes one of the consistent duties of a believer, one who believes in Christ, to expand his or her life in order to receive this faith.

And believing in him is not merely something repetitive: we never finish believing, deepening our faith, handing over to the light and grace of faith our poor soul, our poor heart, our poor life. We need to be capable of a generous act of self-giving, full and complete, and on the other hand we have to be prepared for a continuous effort of believing.

Let us question ourselves a little on the thoroughness of our faith experience We especially who are rather more privileged are accustomed to dividing people into believers and non-believers and naturally we are always included among the believers. And we profess pity, which is not all compassion, for whose who do not believe as much, who find the effort to believe harder, those who perhaps have not yet passed the confines of doubt.

But we too are on the way. We are all pilgrims in faith. We need to make progress, to go ahead, and this is the path of conversion. It is a path which makes us more humble, more open to the truth, and especially one which makes us more able to understand God's mercy by ourselves becoming merciful.

The tax collector Zacchaeus, believing in Jesus, who told us not to judge, had found himself suddenly more friendly and more brotherly, especially towards those who in his life as a tax collector he had not found himself able to treat as brothers. It is through faith in Jesus that he receives the gift of another aspect of conversion and comes to the way of justice and charity.

By believing in Jesus we are helped to grasp, beyond human convention, what justice is: respect for God's laws and respect for God's creatures. Not a justice seen solely as formal law but a justice which is first of all an enlightened view of people God loves and associates with his designs.

Zacchaeus had an account to pay with justice. He had robbed, he was a thief, and now he has been convicted. First he thought to be simply a rogue well able to control worldly matters, turning them to his own advantage (and how much human justice comes down to that). But now he says to Jesus: "I will restore fourfold."

This person who believes in Jesus becomes just: we can apply it to ourselves too. As we well know, the demands of justice are not payable in money only: there is the dignity of the human person, consideration for weakness and frailty in others, acknowledging God's gifts, a whole personal dimension of justice to which we have to be converted.

It is unjust to judge others: only God has the right to judge. It is unjust to betray the truth in our dealings with others, because we are born to bear witness to the truth. It is unjust to have a hard, unfeeling heart in the face of all the various forms of human suffering, in individuals and in society.

Checking on our justice

Also concerned with this justice, I believe, should be our examination of conscience, to check on how we stand with our conversion. It has almost become the fashion to feel required to judge others, not only as a right but as a duty. We seek to be objective, realistic, concerned, consistent, but this is a vocabulary we use without compassion, without love.

We should make an examination of conscience and, enlightened perhaps by a renewed gift of faith, realise there is so much to put right in our life, which is characterised by the spirit of the world and a culture not only secularised but deadening hearts and minds. More especially, we feel ourselves to be judges rather than accomplices. And yet we are brethren, we all share responsibility. We should pardon one another because the Lord pardons us. And that is justice.

Finding the fulness of charity

The tax collector understood all this when he met the one in whom he believed. And it is not at all strange that from this so very thorough comprehension of the demands of justice there developed that fulness of charity which crowned his conversion. Not only did he restore what he had wrongfully exacted but he distributed his wealth to the poor. It is charity which judges not, which forgives, which embraces fraternally, which gives and knows the joy of giving without knowing in the doing of it pride in the ability to do it.

It seems to me there is enough here for a somewhat out of the ordinary examination of conscience, a little less superficial, a little less scamped. It will be hard if, in making this examen, we do not find ourselves enfolded in the Lord, his grace converting us, his mercy, while it purifies us and makes us worthy of God, making us also meek, merciful, and making us savour the joy of being, with him and in him, profoundly brethren.

And this is true not only in our own intimate being but also becomes true in all of the relationships which characterise our life in community, lived together and harmonised by shared ideals such as consecration, faith in Christ the Lord alone, and our apostolic dedication.

Being converted in community

Perhaps at this point it becomes easier for us to understand that conversion is never a gift made to us as individuals, but a gift which fits us and gives us the skills for living together. It puts into effect the requirement of union as the support of faith and the fulness of charity.

And this examination of conscience on conversion as a gift of the Lord Jesus is also to be applied to actual situations in the religious life. You live in community and too often I feel that fraternal and community life seems to shrivel you and becomes a straitjacket there is a need to get out of. Praying alone is better than together and a personal independent apostolic work is more gratifying and goes better. It is strange that just at this time of renewal of religious life such experiences multiply and prevent our communities from bearing witness to the Lord, and being of total service to him.

We need a little conversion. Perhaps we are a little fuddled with collectivism in so many aspects of life and then find ourselves alone with aridity of heart and sometimes disillusioned. We need to meet Christ when he comes to live in our house and make us see more clearly, fire our being and give all of us that enthusiasm for belonging to him that we have felt so many times and which needs to stay alive and be always increasing.

II
THE HOUSE
OF FRIENDSHIP

Martha and Mary

We have seen Jesus going into the house of Zacchaeus the tax collector, and the welcome he received bearing fruit in conversion. Now we must accompany the Lord to another house: the one in Bethany.

"Now as they went on their way – says the Evangelist Luke – he entered a certain village where a woman named Martha welcomed him into her home" (Lk 10:38). Martha's home is the house of friendship: Lazarus, Martha and Mary. This time Jesus' visit is not directed towards conversion but given over to deepening friendship, fidelity, a relationship profoundly human and at the same time supernatural.

The following meditations are intended to show you how to welcome the Lord as a friend. Indeed for consecrated persons he is the friend above all. He is love. And so we can feel ourselves visited by the Lord, who comes to our house to enjoy a friendship which he offers to us and asks from us.

I understand this friendship in a very strong sense, very profound, very exclusive. We have to remember that 'undivided heart' of which Vatican II spoke. It is proper in regard to the religious life to see this meeting as emblematic of our relationship with Jesus.

Here then is Jesus going into Martha's house. It is curious that Luke does not speak of Lazarus. Evidently it is Martha who counts in this house. We do not know why, but it is always she who does the honours of the house when Jesus comes. In the house is also Mary, and Jesus' entrance into this house – a house of friendship if ever there was one – immediately provokes a reaction.

Martha gives herself to what needs doing, Mary softly softly sits at Jesus' feet and listens to him: one bustles around, the other does nothing. Of both it can be said that they are welcoming the Lord, but each in her own way. Martha is at once preoccupied with preparing a welcome, not only one fit for Jesus but as her heart suggests. And there she is bustling about domestic tasks so spontaneously, in such detail, so suggestive of her preoccupations. So she has given herself to the Lord, received him with open arms, and then got on with her work. And the consequence was that she lost sight of him.

Mary also welcomed the Lord and on the other hand produced a different result: If he is here, all the rest is unimportant; I do not leave him alone but concern myself with him, that is enough. We have here two basically different reactions: Martha is so busy and Mary lets it all go.

Jesus does not interfere. He does not call Martha to sit down and listen to him: she has work to do and he lets her do it. He does not reprove Mary but since she is present, since she is attentive, since she is there, he speaks and Mary listens. Within the one house of friendship these two women welcome the Lord each in her own way.

"Martha, Martha..."

We may think that these two diverse ways of welcoming would both be pleasing to the Lord, and they could have gone on like that maybe, only that at one point the over-busy Martha got a little put out. Stung by jealousy or vexation, she came up to interrupt the Lord. She interrupted, we have to say, in somewhat surprising fashion: "Do you not care that my sister has left me to do all the work by myself? Tell her to help me" (Lk 10:40).

And Jesus who until that very moment had been enjoying the different welcome of the two, when Martha calls him to book replies: "Martha, Martha..." (Lk 10:41). He calls her twice by her name and there is in this repetition a whole bond of friendship and deep understanding. Then after affectionately addressing her like this, he begins by making a statement: Martha is tiring herself out.

It is not a reproof. It is the recognition of the generosity of her bustling welcome: "You are worried and distracted by so many things." Jesus recognises that Martha's solicitude is real, she is not satisfied with sentiments, but translates them into hospitable acts, large and small.

Ordinarily we picture Martha preoccupied especially with the meal, but the Gospel does not say that Martha is only busy about the stove. Rather it was a question of all that eagerness, that temperamental excitement making her rejoice at having the Lord by. It was not as though he does not know it was all done to give him a better welcome, make his stay a more pleasant one, prove to him in all sorts of ways the sensitiveness and generosity of her love and friendship.

But while Jesus recognises all this, at the same

time he reminds her: "You are troubling yourself over too many things." Composed feelings, a reasonable reaction and a simplicity of welcome are here indicated by the Lord as characteristic of true and lasting friendship.

Would Martha have appreciated all the warmth of friendship and goodness in that most gentle reply? Perhaps not, and then Jesus goes on: "Mary has chosen the better part, which will not be taken away from her" (Lk 10:42).

Here we see Jesus playing on faith and affection to prepare the heart to receive the truth.

Two forms of welcome, only one love

What truth? That Mary, by settling herself to listen at the feet of the Lord, has chosen the right place. The Lord feels welcomed by these two women who love him but he stresses the difference in their welcome, a difference which perhaps expresses a different perception.

Martha welcoming the Lord into her house shows an immediate realisation of his humanity. We could say that Martha comprehends all the concrete reality and historicity of the Incarnation: this Jesus is a man and men have their needs. Human beings live surrounded by many cares, many necessities, many problems, which also surface in the deep relationship of friendship.

Jesus is true man and that is just how Martha welcomes him. She allows herself to be involved in the experience of the Incarnation in a very real way.

For Mary on the other hand it is not that she does not see the humanity of the Word. It is not the first time that Jesus has entered his friends' house and it is one of his oases of consolation and peace. But what Mary is able to grasp is the realisation that Jesus is the Word of God and that to welcome him means therefore welcoming the Word, God's Word. That is why her attitude is one of listening: "Speak, Lord, your servant is listening."

It is clear that these two are not opposed, they do not negate one another. No one can say: I take my stand with Mary, or I: stand by Martha. Both of them together tell us in very impressive fashion something precisely on the lines of the friendship, love, intimacy with which we should greet the Lord.

In our house there is room for Martha and room for Mary and we must occupy both places. We must be Mary because we are welcoming the Word; and we must be Martha because we are receiving the Son of man, the Word who became incarnate precisely in order to share the human condition, and from within it to save humanity and the world.

It seems to me that this episode sheds so much light for us and we need to reflect long on it, starting precisely from the conviction that the house is one and Mary's task and Martha's are not alternatives, but dispositions which give full realisation to the welcome that should be made to Jesus.

Luke supplies no other details, but we can believe that Martha was mollified and when she had a moment she too sat herself down to listen, and Mary decided to do the washing up.

It really is a lovely Gospel story and we know how in Christian spirituality it became emblematic, suggesting so many considerations and standpoints for the spiritual life. Also, this Gospel account has had many consequences in regard to the religious life, and some perhaps a little intemperate and excessive, suggested by the two vocations of Martha and Mary as presumed alternatives.

I think that on the contrary we ought to take great care not to separate them. The vocation to friendship with Christ is the vocation of consecrated people and brings these two alternatives together, should bring them together, live them, make them a reality. And it is enough to give a moment's thought to the holy founders, men and women, to recognise that in them the vocations of Martha and Mary are always together.

They are authenticated and nourished by turns, illuminated in turn, and that appears to me to be very important in our day also: no one is called to be solely Martha or solely Mary. We all have to be 'the house at Bethany' where friends received the Lord for what he is, Son of God and Son of man, and loved him and served him as such and bore witness.

Jesus' gift

Receiving the gift

On his visit to the house of Martha, Mary and Lazarus, Jesus' gift of friendship was the most significant and precious part of it. He came to bring something to that house, to give. And Mary's attitude which Jesus defined 'the better part' which would not be taken from her was that very realisation in intuitive love of God that nothing is more important, nothing more precious, than to receive the Lord.

To receive him by drawing from him, seeking to understand his gift and leaving the initiative to him, this was Mary's attitude. It merited Jesus' appreciation because he was sent and had come to be gift: "God so loved the world that he gave his only Son" (Jn 3:16). And nothing pleases Jesus more than feeling himself welcomed, accepted, listened to, understood like that.

The creature's poverty is no obstacle to this gift, nor indeed to this most precious disposition. Poverty of spirit, simplicity of heart, characterised Mary's attitude at the feet of Jesus: she has nothing to do, nothing to say. She has only to receive what the Lord is pouring into her soul and her life.

When John says that love does not consist in the fact of our loving God but that he loves us first (cf 1 Jn 4:10) he is only confirming this stupendous truth. And Mary, when the Lord came into her house, had no thought for what she could offer but understood that he was coming to give, and she understood rightly.

Listening to the gift

But there is a still deeper reason and it is that Mary, putting herself in a listening attitude, shows she understands completely that the Lord is making himself gift as the Word, God's Word and the revelation of his mystery. It is Jesus who manifests the fatherhood, glory, omnipotence, mercy of God and manifests it precisely as the Word made flesh so as to become gift to be seen and heard.

That is, the Word who is from eternity in the mysterious communion of the Trinity, while remaining ever in the abyss of the Trinity, issues by the Incarnation and enters into creation and the human heart as the Word communicating and revealing the Father. Here we are truly at the heart of the mystery.

And does Mary understand all this? Difficult maybe for her mind and reasoning, but with the intuition of faith and love, yes. At the Lord's feet she feels a stream of living water rising within her and she is fed and satisfied. Furthermore, it is Martha who thinks she ought to give the Lord something; Mary knows it is better to open herself to receive not only everything about the Lord but the Lord himself.

Also in considering this, another fact can be seen: Mary is at the Lord's feet, and the evangelist makes no reference to what the Lord says, although we would so much like to know. But the mystery is all in the

action of the one communicating himself to the creature and the disposition of the creature who receives
him. This is the decisive and important thing, not our
foolish curiosity.

Consecrated by the gift

This which is the essence of Mary's experience
should make us think. We say we are consecrated to
the Lord, we say the consecration is our response to
the Lord's action. Theologians argue about which is
more to the point, that the Lord consecrates us or that
we consecrate ourselves to him. Immediately after
the Council there was discussion about the
'*consecrantur*' in the conciliar text, whether it is in the
reflexive or the passive mood.

Mary well knew that it is a passive. She had understood that it was part of Christ's gift of friendship
which, spreading out into her life, made her all God's.
The Lord would remain the Lord, and his giving of
himself to Mary made her consecrated in the fulness
of her being as creature, because creatures exist only
to be filled with the glory and love of God.

Into the simplicity of an attitude which externally
is all silence and inactivity, the mystery breaks
through. Turn over in your mind that marvellous
Christmas antiphon: "While the midnight silence
reigned over all, your almighty Word came down
from his royal throne in heaven" (cf Wis 18:14,15).

Believing in the gift

But the incarnation of the Word which took place
in silence and peace needs to be received. I think we

43

should rightly pause to consider Mary fully satisfied by the Word, filled with the words of God, a surrender wise with the wisdom of God: a surrender participating in the secrets of God known only to the Son.

Do we find ourselves in the mystery of this saving tide?

Let us draw from the gift of Christ's friendship, in the silence of contemplation, before even the fervour of prayer. What emerges from Mary's experience at the feet of Jesus is not what she does but what God does in her. Mary also prays, but later. First she is fulfilled by God's gift.

Mary does not have to say what believing means, she has no need to express her faith in words. Her attitude, completely attentive and open before her Lord, proclaims her faith, a faith which gazes into the mystery, savours it and becomes inexpressible happiness within, ineffable surprise and mysterious enchantment.

Mary is not overwhelmed by God's omnipotence but enveloped by what the Lord is: love, mercy, truth, everyone's life-principle and growth of their very being.

Perhaps when we speak of what we believe we are not always aware of how radical a thing it is: too often our faith is tied to a catechism learnt by heart. But faith is being graced by a gift which is the Word, the Christ of God, which is God, and which becomes ours, fully possessing us, filling every nook with its truth and above all with love.

Contemplating the gift

"My Lord and my God", cried Thomas to the Risen Christ (Jn 20:28). Mary said nothing, totally absorbed in the depth of her spirit, the sanctuary of God and his blessed Word. This is perfect contemplation, the start of an experience which indeed merits the name of consecrated life. It is good to see how far we bear comparison in all of this.

If we think about it, this coming of the Lord into Mary's house to offer her the gift of himself as the Word revealing the Father, is an experience to which we are called. And though it may seem a staggering thing, we ought not to forget that this is a beginning of a friendship with Christ for us.

The mystery of salvation which takes Mary and transforms her, and the stages of her growth in faith, as also the outpouring of her love for God, are not recounted in the Gospel because some things are not to be touched but left inviolate. Mary does not come out of her silence. She is too much lost in her Lord speaking and giving himself to her to find words for her fidgety sister, who nevertheless also shares in Christ's friendship.

All of this can nourish our prayer, not one made up of many words but of silence, when we decide to fix our gaze on Christ as a person and let him transform us. This is why the Father sent him and the Gospel offers us many an occasion for this experience of a transforming meeting with Christ our Saviour, uncreated wisdom become word of life eternal in the never-ending union of love.

The better part

The Lord, replying to Martha who is complaining about being left to do the housework alone, gives an answer which calls for some consideration: "Mary has chosen the better part which will not be taken from her" (Jn 10:42).

In what does this choice of the 'better part' on Mary's part consist?

We have already given a hint of this. In her welcome of the Lord, Mary dedicated herself completely to him: she has, as it were, drawn the most obvious conclusion from the fact that he has come into her house. To welcome him, enjoy his presence, listen to his voice and let herself be filled with his mystery: this is the 'better part'.

Martha is immediately preoccupied with giving; Mary's attitude on the other hand is one of receiving: receiving the Lord. Mary above all, as we have said, accepted the Word of God incarnate, he who brought into this world the revelation and the life of the Father, and this receptive attitude constitutes the whole of Mary's welcome.

But why does Jesus call all this "the better part which will not be taken from her"?

Many interpretations are possible. It may be not a bad thing to stop a moment and scan the depth of truth and grace to be found in this statement.

The psalmist had already said: 'the Lord is my portion'. He is the better part, the children's inheritance and the Father's gift. Here we are truly at the root of the mystery of salvation and it is clear that this 'better part' is not to be set alongside other parts: it is not part of a whole, but the whole.

"My inheritance is the Lord", Mary's treasure is the Lord; and this contemplative woman's intuition which realises she is receiving the Lord as gift is therefore most precious, setting her at peace, establishing her in perfect tranquillity and spiritual joy. She has her Lord, and this gift "will not be taken from her".

It is no passing gift but definitive and lasting. The Lord is an eternal inheritance. Other things all pass away but not the Lord. He remains gift, but it is the guarantee of everlastingness because the Lord comes and does not go away.

Receiving love

It is only this 'part', the Lord, that Mary chooses – and chooses it because it is given – obviously a logical attitude. Let us not forget that Jesus came into that house because they were his friends and it is on the level of friendship that the inheritance has value, the gift becomes meaningful.

Mary receives the gift not so much recognising it

as power and truth, but as a gift of love. She receives Jesus, who is the revelation of love because he alone knows the Father, knows that the Father is love and is sent by the Father to reveal God's love to the world.

Jesus' entrance into this house is in the splendour of self-giving love. Both the sisters love the Lord, and Lazarus too, but Mary's insight is privileged in that it puts things in right order. Mary is receiving in Jesus the revelation that God is love and this love she is receiving as the gift of the very person of Jesus, the incarnate Word.

Here we have the richness and content of contemplation as a freely given revelation by a God who manifests himself as he is. It is a contemplation which has its inexhaustible source directly in the life of the Trinity because the Father contemplates the Son and takes pleasure in him, the Son contemplates the Father, and from their mutual contemplation gushes forth that burning love which is the eternal life of God.

Contemplating love

This eternal life which is God's love is offered continually to human beings, who are called to contemplation. For this has Christ come, for this the Lord visits us, enters the house of our spirit and the depths of our heart and proclaims to us that God is Father, that God is love.

And for us who are consecrated persons, who have desired to give our undivided hearts to the Lord, who want to love him alone, what effect does this declaration of love on God's part have on us?

It ought to disconcert us, not least because it is made to us not once and for all but constantly repeated by the mystery of Christ who came into the world for this. Here is why Jesus tells Mary that 'she has chosen the better part'.

We ought to become more contemplative because we are Christians and our vocation is precisely to enter this mysterious flow of the Trinity which will be our eternal beatitude, and even now should be not a statement which we believe but a life event, a profound experience which pervades our whole being. Truly this woman staying silently at the Lord's feet, who does not move from him, who is filled with the presence of the Lord, has so many things to tell us and we should let her speak.

The one thing necessary

Perhaps our spiritual life answers more closely to a construct we have ourselves created by means of so many categories, however Christian and theological, but responds less to that profound union of the mystery of God revealed in Christ. It is precisely this to which we should be open with a receptive contemplative attitude. We do not have to do many things. We only have to receive and listen to the one who comes. We only have to welcome the one who by giving himself gives the mystery of eternal divine love.

Let us really make an effort to enter into the logic of this 'only one thing'. Our spiritual life is too fragmented at times and we think fervour consists in piling on still more things, even to a mild sort of mania – for everything, for example, to be all biblical or solely liturgical... and we go ahead with our almost unthinking operations, with Martha as our prime exemplar.

We find ourselves more at ease with Martha because she is frenetic and so are we, she is demanding and so are we, she is taken up by many things and so are we. But let us make an effort to make our own the sentiments and disposition of Mary: she stays quiet, says nothing, limits herself to staying put and listening. And yet she has chosen the better part.

Contemplation and action: one single dynamic of love

And this is important for our religious life too.

All the distinctions we have invented about the forms of religious life have almost persuaded us that the contemplative life can be alternative to the apostolic life. The very terminology of the Second Vatican Council and canon law is not even explicit enough in this regard, not for want of clarity of ideas but because faced with the greatness of the mystery. Our human words will always remain inadequate.

There is no consecrated life without contemplation and we ought to put a stop to thinking that the prayer of contemplation is something different from the prayer of active religious; we ought rather to tend towards a unification, a harmonising of the mysterious gift which in Jesus shows us the rationale of God's mystery. Jesus is the Son of the Father, no one is more contemplative than he; but he is also the Son who was sent and no one is more gift, more incarnated, more present in history, more consumed by apostolic dedication. But Jesus on the cross died invoking the Father in a supreme moment of contemplation and dedication incarnate.

All of this should be repeated in our lives, but clearly the dynamic of this mysterious transfiguration starts from the time given to contemplation. In the measure that I realise that God is love, that God loves me first, I become capable of loving, of dedication, an unwearying collaborator with redemption. Action and contemplation are not opposing forces but inexhaustibly fruitful gift from the God who is Love.

The part which will not be taken from us

Jesus said that Mary chose the better part, adding that it will never be taken from her. There is an eschatological dimension to the Lord's remark because the time for contemplation will be that definitive time of glory and eternity, it will be eternal beatitude, the better part not to be taken from us.

The drama of our consecrated life is that we are candidates for this eternal contemplation and in our present life there are a multitude of experiences of it, mysterious foretastes, insuppressible longings which, while they confirm us in God, make us sharers in God's action in giving himself to us, and immerse us in the history of the Incarnation in all the reality of our humanity.

In his Gospel, John calls all of this 'flesh'. "The Word became flesh" (Jn 1:14) expresses the fulness of the gift which God makes to humanity by sending his Son incarnate, clothing him with humanity in its total reality: the human being who is spirit in the image of God, but also a synthesis of creation and therefore flesh and therefore matter. Redeemable matter, destined for resurrection, but still matter.

All this should arouse in us a contemplative disposition, and at the Lord's feet we should grasp this truth and persuade ourselves of it not through our reasoning but because the Lord, incarnating again in us, makes us one humanity conjoined in him. This is the better part which is being offered us and to which we have to remain faithful, and which will not be taken from us.

Contemplation in the night

The Word, by becoming man, had himself undertaken to practise contemplation outside of eternity, in time. He lived always in the presence of the Father, in a communion essential to his life and work; but he also knew fatigue, and his long nights of prayer tell us that to experience God in our earthly state we need nights like his, and that what the Lord teaches in the dark is for us to repeat in the light. We should remember that.

Therefore contemplation is not only joy in the Lord's presence but also being overwhelmed by the Lord's infinite goodness which in our earthly state becomes in us an unfathomable abyss, a mystical darkness.

His agony is a mystical gift which Jesus makes to us. And welcoming the Lord also means taking part in the agony. Shall we ponder this a little? We shall better understand Mary's silence at the Lord's feet, her inner union, composed and at peace. And yet we shall understand that to be welcoming of the Lord has a price to be paid.

We also know that the time of prayer can seem interminable, and then remaining on at the Lord's feet in humility becomes a prelude to contemplation.

This being in silence before the Lord should also become part of our timetable and the times for prayer should be of great importance. If we put ourselves in simplicity before the Lord, the Lord will do something, say something, change something within us, helping us to become more faithful in welcoming him and more generous in serving him.

Incarnation of the Word

After meditating on Mary's disposition in her welcome of the Lord as he enters her house, let us spend some time reflecting also on Martha's attitude.

It has to be said at once that the Lord has been specifically welcomed by Martha (Lk 10:38) and entered that house bearing and receiving friendship. Jesus went to a house of friends and therefore Martha, notwithstanding all the good that can be said of Mary, is no reprobate: she is a friend of the Lord to whom the Lord offers the gift of experiencing his presence.

We have already reflected how Mary's experience was that of an encounter with the Incarnate Word. Hence her attitude of listening, attention to the word, being available to God's gift.

Welcoming the Son of man

Martha, on the other hand, welcomes the Lord differently. This Word in whom she nonetheless believes is incarnate, and this incarnation is neither outward guise nor label, but part of Jesus' identity, the substance of his identity. In his one divine person are the two natures: Jesus is true God and true man, and

Martha by her welcome emphasises in particular attention to his incarnate state.

It is no sin, it is an act of faith, an act which sets her before the mystery of God's loving-kindness. For Martha too Jesus is God's gift, for Martha too Jesus is Saviour, but her perception of his human condition makes Martha closer to us than Mary.

Mary, overwhelmed by the presence of the divine Word, feels that the only thing to do is to dispose herself to receive, to listen. Martha on the other hand, receiving the Word but as incarnate, in his suffering state, hungry, thirsty, understands that here is a friend to whom she must give.

It is reasonable for one who loves him to see to his needs. Martha is fully taken up with this idea and so she sets about it: she tidies the house to make it more attractive and welcoming, is concerned for him personally – he will be thirsty, hungry, tired – in short, she sets going all the responses which are the usual expression of human living and conviviality.

It is not by chance that it is she who welcomes him in, and this human side of hospitality is characteristic of Martha: it is human warmth offering to supply for human need in another, in this case Jesus, presenting himself to her in his humble, human necessity.

Loved for loving

This relationship is essential also for anyone believing in Jesus: we cannot do less and pretend that Jesus is true God only. To welcome him in his full identity is part of our faith and the acting out of our faith. When we speak of love for Christ we must not remain in the clouds, we have to be realistic. Like Martha. She responds to this Jesus, the gift God makes us out of love for us, by busying herself with giving.

That is what Martha experiences. Her need to give is a little agitated, a little hasty perhaps too, but are not these first reactions of her love? Also human love for the Lord has to find the right road, an un-ceasing process of interiorisation, and needs gradu-ally to be purified of a certain sensible and emotive effervescence which is not wrong but must be kept in order.

A human being is, before all, spiritual and in the image of God and must therefore settle down to that serenity, simplicity, and that serious dignity in loving which are qualities of God's love.

Towards a love worthy of God

Here we can see in Martha something of ourselves. Called to love Christ by giving him all, ourselves, our life, our days, our time and energies, we need how-ever to go forward in this loving task of giving in such a way that we, little by little, open up to the incarnate Word, and this will put us in accord with our true nature which is being made new and mature by Christ for eternity, where all these ferments will come into new and glorious harmony.

In this attitude of giving with which Martha re-ceives her Lord we sense the fervour of charity being purified. We have to love God in God's way; we have to become capable of going beyond our much reason-ing, our much thinking, all our feeling and desiring, and arrive at that tranquil possession of love of God which, while being offered to us as gift, is still for us a long road to travel.

And we have to realise how the wealth of humanity within each one of us – differently composed for each one, since the Lord never repeats himself – is going to be raised up by our welcome of Christ and the love we give him.

The possibility we have here means that anyone with intelligence must put it all to understanding the Lord, knowing and loving him; anyone who is a poet must write poems for the Lord; anyone with a voice must sing for him. And the ordinary realist must love him with both feet on the ground.

The riches of our human nature are not to be cast aside. But instead of guarding them as our personal possession, instead of turning them to our own account, using them to come out on top, we have to put them at the Lord's service.

But we must humbly recognise that our human qualities, our resources, which are indeed the material for our giving to Christ, for our loving and serving him, are qualities which need to be elevated in order to become worthy of the Lord: by our ability to preserve them for him, offer them to him, spend them, put them totally at his service.

They need to be refined and educated. We need to rid them of a certain impetuosity, vehemence, intemperance; we must free them from a certain kind of laziness, so that our gift of ourselves may be worthy of the Lord. We can see this in Martha who gave all, but her giving is hasty and a bit pushy, even to the Lord: "Do you not care that my sister has left me on my own?" (Lk 10:40). And the Lord gives her some instruction: "Martha, Martha..." (Lk 10:41).

Jesus' teaching method

Let us recall another occasion when Jesus met this family (Jn 11:1-44). When Lazarus was dying they sent to tell Jesus: "Lord, your friend is sick", and Jesus acted as we know: first he delays, then he goes and there follows something similar to his other visit to Martha's house. She goes at once to meet him and says to him: "If you had been here, my brother would not have died."

In these words there seems to be a little of that assertiveness, so human and generous, which characterises Martha and makes her engaging. Jesus does not reprove her; he asks: "Where have you put him?" and it is Martha again who says: "But Lord, it is four days now!" She has an extremely realistic view of things; she is a prisoner, so to say, of the inexorably concrete nature of human situations.

And Jesus brings Lazarus back to life, returns him to the embraces of Martha and Mary, and once again restores the profound mystical balance of friendship which binds him to these women.

It is not a question of our denying our humanity but of purifying it; not a question of betraying God's gifts but of making them worthy of him in our actual conduct, so as to present ourselves to him as his children and his friends.

A path of friendship

Friends, yes. It could be said that Martha treats Jesus with a marvellous simplicity, as she would an older brother. Even when she is a bit annoyed by her sister's attitude, she does not refer to her but to Jesus. At the death of Lazarus she acts in the same way and this strikingly human way of behaving is something I think we should consider, because we are called to be friends with the Lord in the context of our humanity. Called indeed to resurrection but for the moment still on the road. Mary is in advance of us on that road because the Lord has put her a little ahead, but Martha goes along with us.

Chastity, poverty, obedience: roads to community

All this appears to me to be good and fine too for our religious life, in which the closeness of human relations undergoes a profound transformation. The evangelical counsels of poverty, obedience and chastity are not a denial of our humanity but they order it in a different way.

Chastity does not wither the heart nor mutilate it but makes it undivided. Which has its difficulties, its roads to travel, its setbacks, in order to arrive at a capacity for a love purified of all hazy sentiment.

Our poverty puts us in a different relationship with all the good things of the earth. This is because the conditions of our life are more cut off from the temporal, being located rather in the eternal, while remaining profoundly human. And here we have to overcome contradictions, have to find the right balance, and this is a progression, and on this road we mature when our love of Christ is a living love and when, above all, we make sure that the Lord never leaves our house.

And so, even in matters of obedience, interpersonal relations come to be firmly based on respect, which is connected with the dignity of the human person. At the same time we come to be freed from egoism, arrogance, ambition, self-love. Everything gradually flows into a truer, deeper fellowship which allows us to remain ourselves and, through the gift of divine adoption, to become more close to one another in a mutual charity, with a new capacity for goodwill towards others and for community living.

Christ is among us as a sacrament of friendship which denies nothing of what is humanly good but transforms everything into God's family relationship, where the Father and the Son are continually the source of radiant eternal life.

The story of Martha and of Mary is from this point of view truly symbolic, and we should take care not to set one against the other but perceive them to be necessary to one another, because both are authentically themselves.

Experiencing our poverty

Counting the cost

We have been considering how Martha, solicitous in her welcoming of the Lord, is wholly taken up with generous giving. This task, which is her expression of faith and love, she carries out with the natural impetuosity characteristic of her and a heart full of feeling and ardour.

But it remains true such love is costing and here it is that Martha experiences weariness, limitations, poverty of resources. We too often discover that we do not know how to receive God's gift well nor how to give the Lord what he is asking of us at the time.

This alternation between experiencing poverty of giving and poverty of receiving marks our whole life, and our insufficiency becomes increasingly perceptible to us because our vocation makes us seek to be more fully faithful to the Lord, nearer perfection and more worthy of him.

Giving for our own sake

To return to Martha, we see her flustered and running hither and thither and the Lord checks her:

"Martha, Martha, you are concerned about too many things." He is not rebuking her but showing her by this that he has seen, has understood and appreciated her efforts. At the same time however this observation from Jesus helps Martha to realise that her flurry over the many things to be done is indeed generosity which the Lord appreciates, but also a human imperfection which the Lord wants to correct.

Jesus has recognised her love, but has found overwork to be an expression of dissipation, distraction, giving attention to things which do not merit it, and especially a siding of the actual situation she is in at the moment. First has to be the Lord's presence in that house, and then all the rest. Mary has understood this but Martha on the other hand risks overlooking it. And so she is experiencing poverty and fatigue in giving: her confidence wavers, her presumption of being able for everything weakens.

Recognising our limits

It is a spiritual experience which repeats itself in our life, especially in our apostolate, our call to be dedicated to the Lord and to others we want to save with him and for him. We can see that paying in person, wearing oneself out, is costing and often we react to this experience in our apostolic labour with a proud: "I've got to do it!", rather than with admission of our powerlessness, our incapacity, our limitations.

The age in which we live is a time when apostles are tempted more to omnipotence in their reactions than to slackness in their work. We are very close to that vision of superman to whom nothing is impossible: progress, culture, technology can do all. And I am not sure that some of this 'pride of life' has not entered into our hearts, our plans, our undertakings. We are all a little tainted with omnicompetence, omnipotence, self-sufficiency.

"Martha, Martha, you are concerned about too many things": let us allow the Lord to say this to us. He does not start off on academic discourses, does not theorise, but calls us by name and as a real friend, tells us it is not true that we can do anything, give unendingly, it is not true that with our mental equipment, cultural or technical, we can overcome every difficulty.

God's omnipotence in our limitations

When Lazarus fell sick Martha sent for Jesus in the hope that he would arrive in time before her brother died. According to her, later would be too late. Jesus however arrived in time to teach Martha that what was humanly impossible he could do. This is Christ's teaching method, which helps his friends to change direction and start to follow him.

When Martha experiences something of her limitations, fatigue, poverty, she rather becomes impatient and goes off to Jesus. We on the other hand shut ourselves up in the realisation of our insufficiency, our poverty, our tiredness and do not find our way to the Lord for him to supply a remedy.

Perhaps then we will meditate on what Jesus is teaching us as he did with Martha: not to let our life be shattered, its basic unity split apart, fragmented by a self-dedication which does not put the Lord, his presence and his omnipotence in first place.

At the end of the Lord's lesson, accepted with serene and tranquil humility, I think that Martha went back to her work with renewed spirit, with a new understanding of herself and of the Lord. May it be the same for us. Sweetness in giving ourselves to Christ is necessary to the purity of our love but also for any credibility that love is to have.

We find so often that in spite of all our striving, all our giving, people do not believe us, are not moved, have no sympathy. Why? Because our dedication is often rashly clothed in presumption, peremptoriness, self-sufficiency. Then there is need to think, meditate and pray, and seek to benefit from the lesson which comes to us from Martha who admitted to the Lord that she was poor, weak, powerless.

The weight of our humanity

But there is something else to notice. Martha's distraction is not produced by heavenly things which she believed in but set on one side and forgot for the moment. It is produced by earthly things which for the time were preoccupying her more than was right. It was the things of this world which were ensnaring Martha as they ensnare us, for we are in the world, we are flesh as well as spirit, body as well as soul.

Earthly things all have a relative density and block out the light, and until we are in glory this obscuring of heavenly things and this diminished transparency of earthly things we have a hard job to reverse. All of us.

Shall we consider a little this burden our humanity has, which we too carry in our dedication to Christ, and from which we need continual purification? This is the spiritual path to that fulness of friendship with Christ for which we shall have no heart and no courage except in him.

To keep company with Martha can, then, be a

useful exercise: she is a woman Jesus bound to himself by strong ties of friendship, but she had to pay for that friendship, work for it, live it with generous dedication and also with all the purification the Lord put her through.

We have to convince ourselves that friendship with the Lord has demands so transforming and transfiguring as to put us continually in crisis, and Martha's sanctity then becomes an example for us as consecrated persons. Truly a form of sanctity with a supreme definitive expression of love of Christ and for Christ, but one which takes us along a whole road of purification and self-denial.

These are some thoughts which can help us to pray, help us in our examen and also lighten and fill with joy our holy vocation and our duty of loving and bearing witness to the Lord.

God alone suffices

In our meditations we have met Martha in her dedication and her generosity experiencing poverty.

And how did Martha react to feeling overwhelmed by the many things in which she is involved by the generosity of her heart and the confusion of her feelings? Did she lose courage? No, she realised she was poor, incapable, but she was not discouraged. Did she take it out on her sister? That would have been the expected reaction, the most obvious, but Martha is considerate of the Lord: she is a good creature and finds another solution.

To Jesus to find peace

She realises she had been wrong in leaving Jesus and now she goes to him; she is upset but she still has complete faith in Jesus, and trust too, and so here she is confessing to the Lord: "Do you not care that my sister has left me on my own?" (Lk 10:40). There is a loving undertone to this query, worth stressing. However, the important thing is that she has found the right road.

Experience of her poverty has led her to Jesus and Jesus welcomes her with a benevolence worthy of the friendship he has for her. But for all he welcomes her he does not accede to her request, does not fall in with the same way of thinking as Martha: he helps her, corrects her, strengthens her, confirms her most amiably: "You are worried and distracted by many things" (Lk 10:41).

Perhaps Martha found herself captivated by these words and her relations with Jesus became more profound, more frank, more in the light of truth. The Lord told her he knew she was overworked, reminded her she should not be exaggerated in her solicitude, because her being worried over many things did not win his approval: one thing is necessary (Lk 10:42).

This attitude of Martha's, discovering her poverty and going to lay it in the heart of her Lord, is meaningful for us too. Where do we go when we have too much to do? Who do we pour it all out to?

Martha had gone to Jesus conscious of her poverty and this seems to me to be the contemplative side in her. Here now she is not the general manager, she is the one who understands the Lord, enters into the logic of his mysterious love and loving-kindness. And that is pleasing to Jesus.

Contemplation in Martha

So it is true that Martha can teach us something very important for our life, which has to be continually reconciling the requirements of a Mary and a Martha. We can never be Mary to the extent of neglecting Martha and vice versa.

The Lord comes into our house, comes to tell us the things of the Father, gives us heavenly things, concerning salvation, and we have to be ready to welcome him. Nevertheless we have to consider our human capabilities however purified by grace. We should not be envious of those who succeed in being more immediately Mary than Martha, nor of those who succeed in being more Martha than Mary.

The gift is the same each time: the Lord who comes. The gift is his love, the gift is salvation. The rest is the personal story of each one and none of us has the right to think that our Lord is best because none of us has the right to call the Lord 'ours'.

That is how it was with Martha and Mary: the occasion for welcoming the Lord, their service and love of him each lived in the profound difference of her human identity, but also in the profound conjunction of her own mystery with the Lord's gratuitous love: the Lord loves first and is the first to give himself to his creature.

This is the basic condition in our life, a condition to which are then added the most diverse life-histories with the most contrasting events. But it is one which demands that we should be faithful in our receiving and giving to the Lord, in the full use of those gifts of nature and grace which the Lord has given to us.

Reconciled to ourselves

So Martha could go back to her activities, perhaps with a greater intensity of love and fidelity, and now the two sisters are at table with Jesus. The contrast between them has disappeared, the antithesis has gone. They have the Lord there, they listen to him, are nourished by him, filled with happiness and blessed joy.

It still remains true that the two sisters see Jesus

through different eyes. But the Lord allows himself to be enjoyed, possessed, served by these two women, reconciled in undertaking their respective service.

We too can be seated at that table because the Lord's love is so great that the more it is given the less it is divided. The more it is given the more of itself it reveals. The wider it becomes the more it becomes the story of a redeemed humanity and creatures loved as he alone knows how to love. I think the experience of this to be one of the most beautiful things in our consecrated life, a life which should be open to receiving the mystery and welcoming the message so as to be graced by that same gift.

The 'too many things' in our life

We must not however forget that Jesus reproved Martha for taking on too many things. That 'too many things' accuses us also because this is one of our most frequent experiences. How many things, too many things! And the Lord who is glad to be at our house, happy to sit at our table, reminds us that this 'too many' is not done for him. The Lord asks us for our all. But he does not ask for too many things.

It might seem that in saying these words Jesus is referring to the too many material things occupying Martha. Instead he was referring to those things which make us forgetful of him. This is the tiresome experience we often have. It will not do to arm ourselves with clocks and diaries to put order into these 'too many things' since their function is precisely to fragment us, divide us up.

We are so caught up in the too many things that even when we are tired of them it is difficult to know how to free ourselves. But there is worse to come:

instead of freeing ourselves from the things that are too many we free ourselves from those which are never too many. This is an experience which needs emphasising if we are to understand ourselves.

The 'too many things' are this world's realities, and not only the material ones but also the spiritual, to which we give heed not with the priestly intention of an offering to the Lord but to find in them our satisfaction, our gratification. We follow what we want rather than what the Lord wants and take it for granted that what pleases us also pleases him.

This crowd of things in our apostolic life, our work, needs to be examined, be put before the Lord, since it is for him to choose, to decide, and thus for us to be freed of all the things of this world to which we engage ourselves.

We connect with sensible things through the senses, and the immediacy of this experience risks making them the first things to come into our minds even when we are concerned with the things of God. Then precisely is there need for the Lord to remain living and present in our life, for him himself to make the choices. To submit our choices to be sifted by faith so as to thin out the too many things, so as to tend towards the 'only one thing' of which Jesus spoke to Martha, that appears to me to be an unending course to follow in our life.

The virtue which makes us free

We can grow old in the religious life, keep so many jubilees, but in this respect it could be said that we experience the fact that as we grow older we put down roots here more than up above.

"Martha, Martha, you are worried and distressed

about many things"; let that be said to any of us closed in on our little spiritual world, our relationship with Christ, our apostolic task, in a word, the course of our religious vocation. And the sole guiding principle which can help us get free is the presence of Christ. We have to attend to our scale of values: only one thing is necessary, God alone suffices.

Then we shall realise how this visit from the Lord, this inviting in of the Lord, becomes a journey of purification, a spiritual liberation. For we are on the road with Jesus to reach contemplation of the Father. This contemplation will be made up of mysterious silences but rich in light, truth, communion, peace.

This is the road we have to travel and Jesus' call to Martha provides sustenance for our journey. It acts as purification and finally transfiguration. On Mount Tabor, Peter cried: "It is good for us to be here." Nothing is of greater importance, nothing has greater value.

The experience Martha and Mary went through was similar and it has much to say to our spiritual life.

We should accept this and ask ourselves why in our life the longing for heaven and the mysterious intuition of Christ's love are so rare and so quickly fade. Perhaps we too merit Jesus' reproof to the disciples on the road to Emmaus: "How foolish you are, and how slow of heart to believe!" (Lk 24:25). They were with Jesus and did not know him, were walking along with him and did not recognise him.

The saints are alive to these things, they perceive them and remain witnesses accusing us. For there to be upheavals in our spiritual life which move us to the depths, shafts of light which bear us heavenward, delightful moments of communion is something which should occur. And even if we never go into ecstasy, we should meet the Lord, know and love him, should feel his transfiguring embrace.

Do we think of this? We ought to question ourselves before the Lord. "Lord, do you not care?"

We need to know how to live with the Lord and find that familiarity the saints enjoyed. In Martha and Mary it became a symbolic experience always there to give us such hope, throw light on so many paths and console so many desires and aspirations after holiness.

III
BECOMING INTEGRATED

The will of God

To Martha who asked to be helped the Lord gives a reply which merits further consideration. He tells her that only one thing is necessary and invites her to dedicate herself completely to that one thing, or better, to make of that inextricable jungle of things to be done, one single thing.

He asks of her an effort at integration so as not to be divided and fragmented.

It is clear that Jesus' request did not mean that Martha was to be continually thinking: I do this and I don't do that, this yes, that no, in a casuistry of fidelity difficult to determine and quantify. Rather, she was invited to an inner transformation.

The many things

We too have to become aware like Martha of our dissipation and fragmentation: so many things to be done. And how often we think that our generosity of spirit and our service of the Lord and his glory have to be measured by how many things we do, the various tasks we perform, so that we never manage to come to a stop in the oppressive drive of our days.

"Martha, Martha, you are troubled about too many things." Jesus too was besieged by the many things: everyone came round him, wanted him, asked for wonders and signs and words; but in the midst of all this he had something else which kept him integrated: he always did the will of the Father. The various material things to be done did not dissipate him in multiplicity because in everything Jesus always did only one thing, the will of the Father.

The 'only one thing' of which the Lord spoke to Martha follows along the same line. His intention was not to exhort her to be less generous in her gift of herself, less attentive to the calls of charity and service. He meant her not to be wrapped up in one thing after another, always something different. He wanted her to anchor herself instead in one unchanging task of doing God's will.

If our days are in a state of confusion the fault is ours for not having known how to maintain interior recollection and say in every case: Yes, Father. And when now and again the multitude of things crushes us we not only become less Christian, but also less those creatures God has put at the head of creation to raise it up to him, not for us to let ourselves be trapped, torn, impoverished.

To bring unity into our life is the spiritual task we should pursue by reason of grace and in the light of faith, but above all with the growing conviction that the Lord loves us and expects our love in our daily life. Love of Christ brings fidelity to the will of God, lifts us up and associates us with his constant doing of God's will.

We should accustom ourselves never to lose sight of these points of reference which enlighten, give con-tinuity, and little by little unify us, psychologically as well. And all this we can do by perseverance in our task and fidelity to interior recollection, a right intention, and a generous offering of all to the Lord.

This is not to run away from reality but to discover that precisely through unification of our fragmented nature human realities can become a part of doing God's will.

Everything is passing, the Lord remains

The whole whirlwind nature of the things which so wearisomely fill our days is also an indication of their frailty: things pass away. We must be open to a consideration of their vacuity, their precariousness and provisionality. But if everything passes, inevitably everything also comes along.

Perhaps this passing of things is also the Lord's coming? Perhaps also a continual call to take our stand and anchor ourselves in him who never passes away. We are in the Lord's service and must do things out of love by showing willingness, by offering him what he calls us to at that moment.

The criterion for evaluating the importance of our gift is the will of God: when the Lord asks us for something, we have to give him that thing and not another we choose in accordance with plans of our own making which we rarely follow through.

"In your will is our peace", says the psalmist.

To be at peace in God's will: what a beautiful spiritual experience. Here is the door, here is the harbour; and to take God's will as the guide for life is the one care of a consecrated person, called to be with Martha and Mary. It is the duty of living in peace and inner serenity, even if we do have to strike a balance between passing things and the lasting stability of a reality which is not passing.

Do we realise things are ephemeral?

In this connection I should like to point out three lines to follow in an examination of conscience, adapted to people who are inevitably marked by the customs and culture of our time.

Let us ask ourselves: What part does love of Christ have in my life?

Is it a set phrase or an ever more living and profound experience?

Is the Risen Christ something in the past, or remote? Or is he a presence challenging me because it is to this Lord I owe love and fidelity, and who has promised to remain with me always?

On the other hand let us also ask ourselves: Are we really persuaded of the passing nature of things? Are we persuaded that earthly realities are fleeting? or are we tainted with the false realism which holds only the things of this world to be convincing, those things which can be observed and tested? From our response to this question will then also derive the whole hierarchy of values which are our inspiration and by which we live.

Finally, let it be often said that the things of this world are good and to be enjoyed, as God's gifts. But that absolutising of the things of this world as goods to be unconcernedly consumed, how is that to be reconciled with the mystery of the cross and redemption revealed to us by the Lord and to which we are called?

These are questions also which should become a striving for renewed fidelity to Christ the Lord in love and delight in his friendship. Jesus came into this world in order to take us with him to the Father, and if along the mysterious ways of salvation we must lose all things, let us remember the words of the Gospel: "Those who love their life lose it, and those who hate their life in this world will keep it for eternal life" (Jn 12:25).

In the presence of God

Reintegration

The ideal of shaping our life so fragmented on the surface by the multitude of things and developments into a substantial unity is still an ideal to pursue. We should realise that it is no easy ideal. On the theoretical level it is fairly straightforward to convince ourselves that indeed we cannot segment our lives but must consolidate our inner identity, precisely through this unification of ends and coordination of means by which our life must be sustained and developed. In practice we recognise that we are extremely vulnerable and prone to distractions.

Talk of distractions in the spiritual life used to be fairly common: from the standpoint of a classic asceticism, overcoming distractions was a duty and an exercise. Today we are uninhibited. To us there appears a necessity to be always thinking about a hundred and one things and that to the extent that it comes to be almost pleasurable.

We have however to realise that from a spiritual perspective this continually changing succession of change of programme, change of outlook, change of imagery, change of experience, exhausts us, empties

85

us, diminishes us. We are increasingly less ourselves and arrive at the point where we no longer know where we stand at all. To bring about unity to such a way of living becomes a most complicated and at times hopeless undertaking.

God present

But are there any avenues which can help us to bring unity into our life and the lives of others?

It would not be a bad thing perhaps to try to find some answer to this question. And the answer to hand is again the story of Martha and Mary.

Martha and Mary in their different fashion held on to a reality: the Lord's presence in their house. Neither of the two lost sight of this fact. They focused their attention on the Lord's presence however differently. This gave unity to their existence, and the 'only one thing' of which Jesus spoke, took over their lives.

So, for personal integration the fundamental necessity is to live in the presence of God. To live always in God's presence, to act in such a way that one's very life unfolds under God's gaze, has in the history of Christian spirituality been one of the most accepted requirements, most sought and most often realised.

It is true that we are always in the presence of God, it is true that God not only sees us at every moment but is within us, and this presence of his, deep within our existence, is a real, concrete gift. But it is important to take note of it because so often there is the risk that this mystery of the presence of God in us is dimmed in our inner consciousness. It is not unusual to hear it said: "We should live as though we were always in the presence of God" or "We must think that God sees us."

'As though we were.' But we are! And so it is, whether we think of it or not. This objective presence of the Lord within and around us is forcefully expressed by the Apostle Paul in his address to the Athenians: "In him we live and move and have our being" (Acts 17:28). And the psalmist ponders: "If I ascend to heaven, you are there; if I make my bed in Sheol, you are there" (Ps 139:8).

This is true. But the problem is not so much to establish the truth of it as to conclude that if God is present we should live in his presence, should be nourished by his presence and enlightened by his presence.

Hence then the very varying dispositions of those wishing to live in the presence of God: one goes into solitude, in isolation from all creatures; another is lost in the contemplation of nature, the voice, the blessing and wonderful manifestation of God. This is not the important thing: what is important is that the various life experiences are conducted in the Lord's presence.

And the Lord is present in the glorious transfiguration on Mount Tabor as he is present when giving up his crucified spirit. He is present in the marvellous manifestations of his epiphany, he is present in the invisible interior promptings which surpass our way of seeing and hearing and which we know to have come from him. So, I can find myself saying that the Lord has spoken to me, his voice came to me, his inspiration has guided me.

An enfolding mystery

The presence of God is a great mystery which enfolds us, in which we live and move and which gives unity to our life because the presence of God is not a variable: it is invariably present. If I believe in it then I am living in the presence of God and that unifies me. The orientation, motivation, destination of the things I do, undergo, enjoy or receive remains this presence, and the multiplication of things in my life will signify a multiplication of calls from this limitless God.

I have to allow him the right to be present in many ways, precisely because the infinity of his presence is in some way perceptible to me only through the variety of things. Then my fragmented days, my time all in a rush, the many limitations of my life, come to reveal the Lord's presence.

If I tune in to this mystery I live in the presence of God and I stand in the presence of the living Lord. If we take seriously this conviction and certainty we can come to a living experience of what a job it is to withdraw from the Lord's presence.

And perhaps it is not a bad thing to tell ourselves that the fact that the Lord is present to us is much more important than our being present to him, and we ought to receive this most sweet and splendid reality as indeed a fact. When we speak of the ubiquity, the immensity, the infinity of God we are not referring only to a series of metaphysical concepts relating to him but to an historical dimension of the mystery of God.

The creation of the world and the history of salvation bear the stamp of this presence and we may ask how, this being so, we can ever find it so hard to set to, let ourselves be involved, and say to the Lord:

You take the initiative to be present
and I do not withdraw,
I welcome you in.
I realise that in accepting you
the limits of my poor being

are strained
because you are infinite and eternal.
And yet I know that you have made me to
    receive you
and contain you.
I only need to accept
that your measure should become mine.
You do not rob me of anything, Lord,
by so doing. You give me all.
It is enough that I humbly confess
you are all and I am nothing,
you are the Lord and I a creature,
you are Being and I non-being.

The living God in whose presence I stand

We have to let these thoughts sink into our life for them to be true in the everyday, our own ordinary day-to-day. We should think them over and make them become the mystical norm of life, the expression of faith, the work of love, a living in the presence of God, a following of that Lord who invades our very being to the core.

But believing in this mystery, letting ourselves be captured by it, is not enough. We are creatures of consecutive motion, limited in our possibilities and regulated by our time schedule, and this crowding of time, with its invasive obsessive rhythms, shows that in order to perceive the Lord's presence we have to train ourselves. We have to work at it.

Christian ascetic wisdom has always attached much importance to various small practices of the presence of God. The striking of the hours are a reminder that God is near. The rising and setting of the sun, the whistle of the wind can call out to me the presence of

God and make me feel small before him. Not letting the day's events rattle along one after another as is the way of passing things but offering them to the Lord because they are his. And then there are renewal of intention, attention to good inspirations, interior aspirations made to the Lord.

These are all devices which little by little can free us from the distracting pluralism of the many things, and make us grow in that inner unity which is living in the presence of God, welcoming him and giving ourselves in one essential movement embracing life in this world and in eternity.

A disciplined return to the practice of the presence of God can be most fruitful for making us contemplative like Mary and active like Martha, without being worn out by all we have to do while remaining nourished by him who is the source, the fulness, the blessedness and the glory of our life.

Why not see whether conscious acts of the presence of God along the day cannot gradually become as many as our distractions?

This seems to me an undertaking worth attempting. We can be certain that as by repeated effort we make progress along this route we shall find the presence of God becoming an essential in our lives and so really unifying everything, giving everything meaning and purpose, and preparing us for life in eternity.

There, where there will be no more passage of time, where we shall see God face to face, things will be different, but now there is a need to mature, to grow inwardly. May a little of that grace touch us and a little of that blessedness console us.

Lord teach us to pray

We will now meditate on another work we have to do in order to realise this integration and arrive at the 'only one thing' about which Jesus has spoken. 'One' through the increasingly deep communion with God, one through the on-going simplification of our life from its frequent alternations and one also by that fraternal communion which cannot be lacking in our following of the Lord.

Prayer: a meeting with Christ

We have already taken time to consider the practice of the presence of God as a unifying exercise which brings everything into harmony, makes everything tend towards God and receives all from him. Now I think it will be useful to give a little attention to another work in our spiritual life: our meeting with Christ in prayer.

Basically prayer is a wonderful, solemn unfolding of one's being in the presence of the Lord. To pray means putting ourselves before God, means letting ourselves be touched by his grace and his love and it is to thank, praise and bless him for the mystery of the mercy with which he surrounds us, purifies us.

The prayer of Jesus

Prayer is the breath of communion. Jesus himself gave us the example. He told us that life for him meant to do only and always the will of his Father, and the continual doing of this one thing was sustained by prayer.

We should spend a little more of our time for spiritual exercises in considering Jesus at prayer. He prayed in the temple, in full fidelity to the liturgical pattern of his people, but he also prayed with that personal initiative which the Gospel registers more than once. His withdrawal to pray in solitude underlines how his living eternally with the Father needed to be given concrete historical reality. It must occupy his time, his thoughts, his way of life.

Jesus' prayer is characterised also by a fewness of words which makes for silence. How much time he dedicated to a silent being with the Father, in perfect adoration and full filial abandonment, where obedience found its support. We should be taking Jesus praying as the model for our prayer. So we shall succeed in living in the presence of God, and so make our way through life and follow out our commitment to service and a dedicated apostolate.

The Our Father, school of prayer

But Jesus also made his own pray: master of prayer, he enkindled in them the desire to pray. The Gospel tells how one day the disciples asked him: "Lord, teach us to pray" and we know how the Lord replied: "Pray like this..." (Lk 11:1-2). In the prayer taught by Jesus to the apostles we truly have revealed the amazing richness of Christian prayer.

In it we gather in heaven with the Father ("Our Father who are in heaven") but also mix in human affairs. They are confided to the Father, received from him, put to his service, to create that family of God in which all have affection for each other, all pardon each other, all help each other. In short the "Our Father" is a school of prayer and I believe we should all gain if we attended this school a little more often, as regards our apostolate as well.

So many schools and methods of prayer are stuffed with a confusion of human words, but this savouring of the "Our Father", living its revelation and its gift, is rather left to one side.

A community of prayer

There is another observation I should like to make. In the first Christian community experience, that is, in the gathering of the first disciples of the Lord after the Ascension, prayer suddenly found its fundamental and explicit role. At first it was in fidelity to the prayer of the Chosen People and then, gradually, in giving shape to the celebrations which developed along with the formation of the Christian community and the spread of the Gospel.

It is most striking to see how the Christian community was a praying community. In Paul's Letters precise and detailed attention is given to the community at prayer. This is seen in the way his Letters are rich in canticles, hymns, professions of faith, praise of

God, which still continue to take us into the movement of the prayer of that first community.

Being disciples of the Lord and living with him certainly includes this obligation of prayer, not as a duty but as a profound need deriving from faith and love.

Typifying all this is the episode where the apostles find in their experience of being taken up by the multiplicity of things to be done, the inspiration to divide up ministries and charges to entrust to others, so as to reserve to themselves the service of the word and prayer (cf Acts 6:4). Their decision results precisely from the fact that they found themselves in the same state as Martha and so the division of charges and ministries is born in the Church in the light of the Spirit. The one charge the apostles, the chosen of Christ, could not and would not delegate was that of the word and of prayer.

From this ferment of the Spirit in the Christian community was born also the development of the liturgy. It was in the liturgy that the Church, God's new People, found inspired unfolding of her relationship with the Trinity.

What ultimately brings a praying community to maturity is precisely living the mystery of communion with God. Liturgical prayer by taking up all human concerns into the dynamic of prayer becomes for the community an expression of unity.

Prayer: a foretaste of eternity

To pray is to become united, be in community. To pray is in a certain sense to overcome the division between heaven and earth, anticipating the glory of eternal life.

Here is what we should do and the grace to do it. So we have to seek to join in this wonderful stream of prayer and let ourselves be carried by it. In this way we become participants in a very rich experience which drives away our distractions, purifies our instinctive and egoistical approach to the things of this world, and fine-tunes our communion with heavenly things, making it more intense and more profound.

By praying we enter into the sphere of the eternal, of God, which is redemption and salvation but also blessedness and glory. Praying takes us out of the prison of passing things, out of the fog of earthly transience. Faith becomes more bright, service of the Lord more eager and our continuance in it more assured.

Pray always without wearying

Prayer not only creates a disposition in us but puts us inwardly in tune with the Lord. This spiritual freedom born of prayer should be especially dear to us.

What is meant by 'an undivided heart' is acquired in prayer. Realisation of the demands of fidelity is born from prayer, God's loving claims on us come to flower in prayer, and we should take great care that prayer never becomes less of a reality in our life.

Beginnings in monastic life are from the start characterised by an emerging potential for prayer, seen as a spiritual value in life and therefore also made part of our life-story.

St Benedict has a phrase which is one of the salient points in his Rule, that nothing is to be preferred to prayer – that prayer he defines as 'opus Dei', the essential work of God's service.

Here we should ask ourselves whether, when we speak of our work, we also include prayer in it, or whether we are accustomed to a dualistic view of the spiritual life according to which prayer is one thing and our work another. St Benedict calls prayer *'opus Dei'*: the Lord's followers pray, above all. The rest will be a consequence of prayer and to that they will be faithful. But the great work is prayer.

In all religious orders the subject of prayer is basic.

Now, in our Rule and Constitutions prayer has its place obviously, but there is a need to see if we give our allegiance to that place; that is, whether we are the praying people our rules say we are.

Faithfulness to prayer requires understanding it in the first place as faith: in order to pray we have to believe, and prayer is a journey in faith. But is it? Prayer is a profound experience of communion with God: feeling ourselves loved by him should become a nourishing certainty, life-giving. But prayer should also become our response to that love.

And our own prayer?

This richness of prayer as a way, a personal story, a realisation, a work, we should hold dear, preserve and continually verify. Fundamental to our examination of conscience, the daily practice I hope we still have, should be an inquiry into our prayer. The state of our prayer should be continually tested.

We should oblige ourselves to prayer so that it truly becomes the thing that interests us most, that always takes first place with us, to the extent that *we become prayer* ourselves, channelling all our spiritual powers into the movement of prayer. Our memory and our thoughts are occupied with the mystery of God, our desires are satisfied by that attraction. Our concrete physical humanity too finds more and more the true dimension of creation. It no longer distracts us but proclaims the Lord and is capable of translating us to the blessedness of God.

Clearly therefore that we should keep all the prayer regulations proper to us in such a way as to reverse a certain experience fairly frequent today: we have so much to do we have no time to pray and we end up saying that to work is to pray. That everything should become prayer is undeniably true. That everything will automatically become so because we throw ourselves headlong into things is another matter.

We consecrated people run the risk of becoming impious folk who do not recognise the presence of God in things, who enclose themselves in the intricate web of human events as though God did not have part in it. And so we should cherish a pious disposition precisely as a counteraction. It should characterise our whole life with the sense of the presence of God, submission to God, consciousness of his fatherliness.

Piety was once held to be the fundamental relationship of a son to his father. We can judge the state of our prayer by the intensity of our filial relations with God and our obedience to the Father.

All of this ripens in prayer. And we should make it ripen day by day so as not to become impious like Peter, who merited to be called 'Satan' by Jesus when his way of thinking was not conformable to the Father's designs (cf Mt 16:23). It is only in prayer that our soul learns piety. And that piety is sweetness, mercy, tenderness, communion, repose, anticipation of our life in eternity.

Prayer little by little *frees* our poor human nature from all its rough edges, *frees* our heart from dryness, and *puts us in tune* with God in an ineffable peace, a most precious tranquillity, making us savour how it is that 'only one thing' is necessary.

Walk in love

Prayer is a duty which unceasingly and certainly in a most efficacious way increases our realisation of that 'only one thing' of which Jesus spoke to Martha. We can perform this duty with the intention of putting into effect that saying of Jesus: "Remain in my love" (Jn 15:9).

It is precisely in prayer that remaining in Christ and in his love finds daily food for the journey and experiences the Lord. It is the discovery always new of the wonders of his mercy and goodness. Therefore it is the full ripening of the Christian vocation, which is realised precisely in love of God.

But it must be said that it is not enough to remain in God's love: we need also to continue in his love. Walking in love of God ultimately realises that inner integrity which stops us from being distracted and spread over many things and occupies us with only one thing: the inexhaustible discovery of God's love, the response to his love, and allowing that love to bear fruit.

Keeping the commandments

What does it mean: continuing in God's love? Many things. Jesus said: "If you love me, you will keep my commandments" (Jn 15:23).

That is already a large programme, a long road to integrity, looking to nothing but God's will. It is shown precisely in his commandments. Perhaps we should return to that ancient path of Christian holiness and fidelity to the Lord.

Return to living the commandments of the Law of the Lord not as an authoritarian command but as proof of a love to which we must be faithful.

It is a view of things which we should take up again: "If you love me, you will keep my commandments". And this matter of observance of the commandments is a test which not only lays us open to Gospel authenticity but also makes us authentically evangelical in the deeds of love in our life. What is required is to lead a loving life, returning God's love in all things, turning every event in our life into love of God.

The responsibilities in our life, the 'many things', have to be seen in the perspective of *a God who makes himself present to us*, who indicates what he wants done, opens ways, reveals his plans, and all in love. It is not enough to keep God's commandments literally. They have to be lived in the consciousness that he gave them to us because he loves us and we have to keep them because we love him.

This aspect of love of God is precious because it keeps us authentically in the truth of the Gospel: the mystery of God's loving-kindness which never ceases to manifest itself, reveal itself, give itself, and surrounds us with his grace and mercy.

To walk in God's love has a uniting and unifying effect: uniting us with the Lord, unifying the tapestry of our daily life. It gradually succeeds in becoming our life's motivation.

Why do we do what we do? Why do we spend ourselves on the things we are about? When our motivation is love of God and the brethren an inner peace pervades our spirit and our life.

What is done for love weighs light, becomes a joy. It reveals the grace and beauty within it.

And then spending ourselves, making demands on ourselves, wearing ourselves out, is not just a wearing, emptying, exhausting process but something which enriches, invigorates, gives tireless energy.

At this point we are invited to think whether we do things because we have to, and therefore get sick of them, or whether we do them with love and therefore gain from them.

This also is important in the spiritual life because love is a guarantee of perseverance, of courage, and love also calls out creative powers.

So we are obliged to maintain the concept of charity as explicitly as possible in everything we do. I am speaking of love of God. We should feel ourselves continually enlightened and called, we should continually exercise ourselves in this fidelity to love of God.

It is not enough to say that all is love. We need to put love into what we do. "Where there is not love, put love and you will find love", St John of the Cross used to say. Where we have put it, there it will be, and if it is not there the fault will be ours and nobody else's.

Now, walking in love of God becomes a motive for

ongoing spiritual perfection according to which the important thing is not doing this or that. We do only one thing: we are loved and we love.

This is truly the whole of our vocation: called entirely to the love of God, called to remain in charity, to walk in love and bear fruit in love.

The practice of virtue

In our life, with the increasing number of things to be done, in this tapestry so complex and divided, we are called upon to practise the virtues. Especially those which used to be called the moral virtues: patience, generosity, prudence, fortitude, temperance, mortification, justice.

We should recognise that our Christian life is continually challenged by these virtues. The Lord has shown them to us by his example and proposed them as the norm in his Gospel. But walking the path of virtue is we must admit really hard going.

Patience is all very well, but why must I always be the one to show it? Justice is fine and I have to live according to it, but there is also justice in my regard: I too should enjoy the fruits of justice on the part of others. And so we have a taste of the trials of virtue. In those moments of grace, virtue stimulates us to giving and offering, and at other times drives us into very human weakness, exhaustion, weariness which shows in being a little vexed, dragging along rather, being somewhat depressed.

Where shall we find the integrating strength whereby the practice of virtue instead of being an irksome carrying of the cross becomes a joyous following of the Lord? In love of God.

Virtues practised without love become poisonous. They will poison you.

Virtues practised with love soon become a blessing, and life is unified and harmonious again.

For love alone

We have to take care not to stifle this motivation of living in God's love that we have by too many other motives. If things are not done out of love there is the risk of their being done for other motives which are not loving. Then they lack generosity, verve, and end by being arid.

Think, for example, how day-to-day making some sort of a living has become a problem, everything complicated with forms, accounts, statements.

Altogether we are continually driven in fact by motivations which can become really dehydrating, resulting in the impoverishment of our deepest reserves, with the attempt, and at times it is a temptation, to do things half-heartedly, just enough for them to go on with on their own without too many problems.

I say that from the time we humans arrived at the age of the robot we turned our fellow human beings into robots. We have become cold, dry, calculating, subject to a multitude of annoyances which make our work tiring, stressful.

You will say: but if that is how things are, what are we to do about it? I say that for this very reason we must be watchful, I say that for this very reason it becomes important not to let ourselves dry up, but stay fervent in love of God. Stay sensitive, attentive people, alive, who do not let themselves be stifled by the wearisomeness of things but put love into what they do and experience.

And here, then, we also have the human qualities of gentleness, warmth, the capacity for showing interest and being understanding, to sympathise with others and share their burdens. The need of them is so great.

We should be capable of so behaving that our presence is always welcome. We should be capable of living in our community in a way to be a *persona grata* and not a weight to bear. We should be people capable of foresight, intuition, service, to the extent of being people to turn to in our community.

Let us walk in charity even under its human aspects of serenity, joy, peace spread around us.

And the same applies to our apostolate.

Let us labour, spend ourselves for the salvation of others, and we have to watch that we do it not with dry professionalism but with apostolic zeal. Professionalism if you will, but as a constituent of our working competency not just as our sort of work.

We are charity volunteers. Our professions should not overpower this evangelical dimension and we should guard against hardness of heart. The heart the Lord has given us should remain a heart of flesh. The risk of mummifying it, of turning it to stone, precisely because of the tensions of the many things we have to do, is a risk to which we are constantly exposed.

Only the duty we have of walking in charity purifies us, detoxifies us, makes us people who bear witness to love.

We need to show that we are walking in love, rooted and blessed in love. Because from it spring joy, rejoicing and gladness.

IV
RECEIVING AND SHARING

Following after Jesus

Jesus and women

So far we have been seeking especially to contemplate Jesus in the house of Martha and Mary as he experiences a moment of friendship and welcome.

The Gospel of Luke (6:1-3) gives us another perspective, again revealing as always the mystery of Jesus, and involving his disciples significantly.

"Soon afterwards he went on through the cities and villages, proclaiming and bringing the good news of the kingdom of God. The twelve were with him, as well as some women who had been cured of evil spirits and infirmities: Mary called Magdalene, from whom seven devils had gone out, and Joanna the wife of Herod's steward, Chusa, and Susanna, and many others, who provided for them out of their resources."

Jesus was going from village to village – and this travelling around by Jesus, the Father's envoy, is significantly rich in consequences – proclaiming the good news, the glad tidings that the Father pardoned and saved. He was followed on his travels by the disciples, and this company of disciples is the beginning of God's Church.

The Gospel however underlines another invaluable circumstance, an essential aspect of Jesus' evangelising journeys: some women followed him. They followed because they believed in him, because they loved him and also because they were loved and saved by him.

From the beginning of his mission, Jesus had thought of them, chosen them, made them grow and be with him to the foot of the cross, the holy sepulchre, the upper room and then again and always in the life of the Church.

A faithful loving discipleship

A great deal is said today about the position of women in the Church. The following of Christ is the great journey to which all, men and women, are called and must experience and the female consecrated life gives clear proof of how the following of Christ on the part of women is to be valued. It enriches the Gospel proclamation, above all with the witness of charity.

This I believe is the way to see the deeper meaning of women's consecrated vocation. So many of them saints in God's Church! And is it not continuing in the present? This mystery of holiness is so significant. These women, never lacking in the Church in all ages, merit consideration. They are the ones who have experienced Christ, have discovered the Lord's mercy and tell it in their lives.

Why not give more study to the presence, the history, the holiness and glory of women in the Church down the centuries? This I believe is something which calls for our attention. We all know exemplary Sisters, have met several generous women: why not emphasise this presence, in our community, our parishes, our dioceses?

It is true that the Christian calling of the Carmelite Sisters, for example, does not lead them into great institutional careers but what service, what dedication, what fidelity! We should bless the Lord for it and learn from it.

Consecrated women above all are called to walk with the Lord: accompanying him.

Judging by the Gospel, women were the first to proclaim Easter and this should confirm women in their vocation, make them glad and happy to be women.

Following means confessing

When Jesus came into the district of Caesarea Philippi he asked his disciples: "Who do people say the Son of man is?" The reply was: "Some say John the Baptist, but others Elijah, and still others Jeremiah or one of the prophets." He said to them: "But who do you say that I am?"

Simon Peter answered: "You are the Messiah, the Son of the living God." And Jesus answered him: "Blessed are you, Simon son of John! For flesh and blood has not revealed this to you, but my Father in heaven. And I tell you, you are Peter, and on this rock I will build my church, and the gates of Hades will not prevail against it. I will give you the keys of the kingdom of heaven, and whatever you bind on earth, will be bound in heaven, and whatever you loose on earth, will be loosed also in heaven." Then he sternly ordered the disciples not to tell anyone that he was the Messiah.

From that time on, Jesus began to show his disciples that he must go to Jerusalem to undergo great suffering at the hands of the elders and chief priests and scribes, and be killed, and on the third day be raised. And Peter took him aside and began to rebuke him saying: "God forbid it, Lord! This must never happen to you." But he turned and said to Peter: "Get behind me, Satan! You are a stumbling block to me; for you are setting your mind not on divine things but on human things."

Meditating on this page of the Gospel (Mt 16:13-23), we cannot but be profoundly moved. In fact here the mystery of Jesus is revealed and hidden, is confessed and betrayed, understood and not understood. It gives the very lively gripping proof of how the mysteries of God are greater than we, and of what effort we should make to be open to their light and their grace.

Peter confesses Jesus correctly: You are the Christ, the Son of the living God. He receives a benediction from Jesus: Blessed are you because this has not come from yourself but my Father revealed it to you. But how much did Peter understand?

He understood that Christ is the Messiah, confesses it in the eagerness of his faith and his love, and then? Then he takes him aside, turns into a counsellor of Jesus, and tries to dissuade him from doing what he had said, so as to draw him away from the destiny which the prophets had foretold and which he has every intention of fulfilling. Peter of little faith!

Jesus, faced with his disciple's frailty, is not indulgent as we might wish. With a disdainful gesture he says: "Away from me, Satan, because you do not think according to God." This surprises us too. What

110

can this relationship between Jesus and Peter be, now becoming more compromising and involved?

Once again it emerges how great are God's mysteries and how great an effort it is for the creature to be open to them and accept them fully.

After all, we have to admit that Jesus died on the cross and Peter followed the same fate. So only what the Lord says becomes truth, history, salvation.

And it is in the very reality of this mystery of the saviour Christ that we must find ourselves again, must enter into ourselves with the certainty of faith but also with the task of co-operation, we who are so supported by grace but not delivered from our frailty, our meanness.

Therefore it always remains true that we are saved with no merit of our own and that the gift of faith never becomes an exclusive possession allowing us to boast or making us secure. We have to follow Christ, carrying our own cross likewise, remaining disciples and becoming so more and more.

The Lord gathered his disciples round him as a mark of his friendship, goodness, wonderful election; but what a way they had to go!

If he drew them on behind him, he led them by ways they did not know. He involved them in experiences little likely to disprove the fact that in accepting them he had fed them such words as could scandalise and trouble them.

By his love, Jesus succeeded in carrying them forward and this is a mystery still being accomplished today.

We too are among those disciples.
To us too the Lord has revealed his identity as Son of the Father.

He has told us too that he is the Saviour. To us too he has given words of friendship, loving-kindness, mercy.

To *follow him* has to be the attitude defining our life. In order that our faith shall not be sterile we need to journey on, we need to follow Jesus.

And we know that to follow Christ leads once only to Mount Tabor and so many times to suffering, the cross, sorrows, sharing in the griefs of all and especially to experiencing untiring compassion.

We should be convinced of this and should also realise that the Lord in making us grasp these things is giving us a great grace, an ineffable gift, and planting deep within us his life as Son of the Father, saviour of the world and friend of humanity.

Let us allow ourselves to be conquered, taken captive by him, let us welcome him, listen to him.

Proclaiming the Lord

Again Jesus said to them: "I am the good shepherd. The good shepherd lays down his life for the sheep. The hired hand, who is not the shepherd and does not own the sheep, sees the wolf coming and leaves the sheep and runs away – and the wolf scatters them. The hired hand runs away because a hired hand does not care for the sheep.

I am the good shepherd, I know my sheep and my own know me, just as the Father knows me, and I know the Father. And I lay down my life for the sheep.

I have other sheep that do not belong to this fold. I must bring them too, and they will listen to my voice. So there will be one flock, and one shepherd" (Jn 10:11-16).

The Lord's saying in this extract from the Gospel bears very clearly on the Mass as memorial, extolled by John Chrysostom, famous for his eloquence full of doctrine and passion for Christ and for his life, in which giving in sacrifice had such a place.

I therefore, the prisoner in the Lord, beg you to lead a life worthy of the calling to which you have been called, with all humility and gentleness, with patience, bearing with one another in love, making every effort to maintain the unity of the Spirit in the bond of peace.

There is one body and one Spirit, just as you were called to the one hope of your calling, one Lord, one faith, one baptism, one God and Father of all, who is above all and through all and in all.

But each of us was given grace according to the measure of Christ's gift. The gifts he gave were that some would be apostles, some prophets, some evangelists, some pastors and teachers to equip the saints for the work of ministry, for building up the body of Christ, until all of us come to the unity of the faith and of the knowledge of the Son of God, to maturity, to the measure of the full stature of Christ (Eph 4:1-7,11-13).

St John Chrysostom also made reference to this short passage written to the Ephesians. He was one of the most impassioned and penetrating commentators on the Letter of St Paul, especially on the theme of Christian vocation and the mystery of the Church. It seems to me that these homelies can help us to draw useful instruction from these readings.

And the first thing I should like to underline is this: in God's Church the pastoral ministry of Jesus and the apostles is never ending. Perhaps we are so

accustomed to it that we do not sufficiently realise what a gift this is. Through it God's word is
continually proclaimed, through it the Gospel has
continually borne testimony, and through it by means
of the food of Christ's mystery the Christian community is nourished and helped to become a holy
People of God.

It is right to devote a moment's attention to this.
We religious people are given to emphasising the
shortage of ministers in today's Church and this fact
fills us with pain and concern. We lament that God's
word does not come to us with all the ceremony it
merits, that those with pastoral charge do not take us
by the hand as we might need and desire. We complain, but do we have reasons to complain?

At the least I believe that we ought to realise that
our complaints risk being spiritual greed. In our life
the Gospel is proclaimed: through the liturgy the word
of God is continually offered to the Christian people,
and to us consecrated souls also with particular intensity. Instead of complaining, why do we not seek
to realise to what extent we value the gift of God's
word?

St John Chrysostom did not weary of proclaiming
the Gospel but he wanted that the faithful should
attach importance to that proclamation, take it seriously, not need to have it repeated so many times
before showing fidelity and acceptance.

Paul's text which exhorts us to be worthy of our
vocation is repeated precisely for us: our vocation as
disciples of the Word, witnesses to his Gospel, sharers
in the ministry of the Church is not left unsupported,
without example, without exhortation. But perhaps
we are a little distracted, a little superficial, perhaps
we are a little tired of the routine of holy things and

perhaps we need a spot of persecution, a little real deprivation, a little tribulation to realise how grateful we ought to be to God and his Church for the ministry which proclaims Jesus to us and gives him to us in word and sacraments. May he afford it to us always so that our life may be fed and our fervour, enthusiasm and joy at being Christians are not paralysed by our little daily routines but we discover ever anew the greatness of God's working.

A particular reason for just pride is the fact also that we are not only recipients of a gift but also collaborators in a design which infinitely transcends us but which the Lord's grace, given through our various vocations, renders us capable of proclaiming God, spreading his glory and blessing the Lord.

Let us complain a little less and instead seek to treasure the gift which the Lord continually renews in our lives.

The close presence of Jesus permeates our spirit to proclaim the Father to us, offering us holiness and renewing in us our apostolic mission.

If we consider this we will not complain any more, but rather concern ourselves with employing our gift more faithfully, making it a witness in answer to the most sweet and wonderful signs of the Lord's care for us.

The expressive symbolism of the cross

The Feast of the Holy Cross entered the liturgy through the faithful piety of the Eastern Church and also to emphasise how the Lord's cross is accepted in the Church not only as the mystery of salvation but also as a sign, a relic, a historical testimony to a suffering Incarnation and crucified Redemption.

In other words, the cross emphasises precisely the whole measure of the Incarnation which the mystery of the Word has undertaken for our salvation. Christ has taken on the sorrows of humanity, Christ has immersed himself in the suffering of humanity and by taking it up and making it the essence of his life has also made it the way of our salvation.

And if the Lord's cross has become the symbol of a victorious king it became so precisely by its historical reality and the intensity of human punishment which the Lord knew and the humiliation he accepted in love and for love. The cross was not something symbolic: the Lord truly carried the cross, allowing his shoulders to receive it, his body to undergo the shame and his death to be the death of a wretched criminal, an outcast.

This mystery makes us understand how the Lord Jesus could really be in all seriousness redeemer and saviour. He could well have been a glorious saviour; he willed to be a crucified saviour.

His choice of the cross challenges us. We are saved by one who was crucified, and therefore the Church will always venerate the cross in its very material nature as wood soaked with blood and suffering, and find in it her point of reference.

The cross is the sign of signs, the expressive symbol of all the expiatory realism of Jesus' redemptive work.

We, the Christians of our day, have become lovers of symbols and the cross too is a living symbol for us certainly. But we often multiply signs of the cross as though to compensate for that adoration full of faith we should be experiencing, and above all that following of Christ crucified we should be pursuing.

We have reason for prayer, humility, feeling and

therefore reason for a celebration of the Crucified which would be truly worthy, and make us more able to believe that this wood of the cross is a sacramental sign we have need of not only to preserve and honour but because its grace permeates our life.

The Lord's cross honours the one who bears it: "Those who want to come after me must take up their cross and follow me." To follow the cross means to let ourselves be taken over by the Lord's passion, be configured to him and become ourselves also victims of expiation, an oblation, a burnt offering wholly consumed.

At the foot of the cross stands Mary.

No one could teach us like her how to venerate the cross, how to become witnesses to it and how to resemble it by the commitment and fidelity of our life.

Mary the mother of Jesus

Mary, co-worker with the Redeemer

> Standing near the cross of Jesus were his mother,
> and his mother's sister, Mary the wife of Clopas,
> and Mary Magdalene. When Jesus saw his mother
> and the disciple whom he loved standing beside
> her, he said to his mother, "Woman, here is your
> son." Then he said to the disciple, "Here is your
> mother." And from that hour the disciple took her
> into his own home (Jn 19:25-27).

Mary, Jesus' mother, stood close by the cross.

We are invited to contemplate this mystery which
helps us to understand to what point the Mother of
the Lord is involved in the mystery of salvation and
redemption. She has contributed to this mystery not
only the mystery of her divine and virginal motherhood but also full and total sharing in the way Jesus
took to Calvary.

Jesus sees Mary thus present at the foot of the
cross: he turns to her, takes his leave of her and offers
her another son so that through him her motherhood
may continue and her mission as co-worker with the
Redeemer may become full and perfect.

The mystery of Mary is one with the mystery of Jesus. We have to experience them both at the same level of faith, with the same love, because it is for us that the Father has sent the Son and for us that the Son died on the cross, and through that astounding mystical event Mary is our mother.

Let us never separate Mary from Jesus or Jesus from Mary: they are a part of our faith. Let us never separate our love for Christ from love of his Mother, because now it is for us to crown her with filial love by the fact that we have been entrusted to her by Jesus as her children.

And this profound linking of Mary's presence with Christ's mystery it seems to me should become our first duty in conversion on the level of faith. We should deepen our understanding of this mystery but at the same time we should accept it as we accept the whole of faith. It is not possible to have Jesus separate from his mother, it is not possible to accept the Mother in separation from Jesus, and the reason they cannot be separated we find there, at the foot of the cross.

This means for us that as it is true that we are redeemed by the blood of the Lord, so it is true that we should take refuge in the motherhood of Mary for this redemption to go on deepening and extending. It is Mary who teaches us to welcome Christ, Mary who makes us understand all the demands of this acceptance and fidelity to the redemption. And this includes staying at the foot of the cross, with us also involved in this ineffable martyrdom, carrying the Lord's cross by allowing it to be firmly planted in our life.

Our heart must provide a base for the Lord's cross and our human nature, so in need of redemption, of purification, of transfiguration, must know that this will come about through the mystery of the cross of Jesus and the sorrows of Mary.

If we do this we shall become more generous in the sacrifice entailed by being Christian. We shall become more serene in taking the way of the cross in company with Jesus, more courageous in facing, for the Lord's sake and for his glory, the labours of our apostolic commitment and in being included in that shame, that contempt which Christ experienced in his own person until he could say of himself, "I am a worm and no man."

Christian humility takes on a particular significance today: it contrasts with the pride of life, all the pomposity and presumption in our society, our culture, our dignity. We should let ourselves be brought to nothing by this Lord and perhaps this is the heaviest cross to bear and to understand, but at the foot of the cross we grasp, we enter into, the inexorable nature of the mystery which purifies and illumines all with a fire we should willingly accept.

Let us not be among those who fled from the Lord's cross: we would be fleeing from Jesus and Mary. And where would we go? To perdition and death.

May Mary help us by her faithfulness to her crucified Son to understand the mystery, to love it and live it in the way and in the measure the Lord has destined for us as a sign of predestination and salvation.

Mary, obedient to the Spirit

"Mary treasured all these things, pondering them in her heart" (Lk 2:19).

This is Mary's characteristic attitude: she is the woman who listens, accepts, says yes, allows herself to be led by the Spirit's initiative, illumined by the Lord's word. It is precisely this essential obedience as a part of life that she becomes Mother of the Lord and faithfully generous servant.

We should first of all consider Mary's availability. Mary does not have her own plans, her own arrangements. She greatly resembles her Son: she allows herself to be led, guided, enlightened. Here is one who gives her life and directs the passing of her days along mysterious paths into the full revelation of truth and the full possession of love of God.

This example of docility says something to us too. We too often say we have to be in control of our life. We think it is for us to draw up plans in the short and the long term. We think it is our responsibility as adults and mature people to foresee everything, know everything, deal with everything. But is that right, in fact?

Is it right when this preoccupation which is so human often ends by preventing us from letting God be the important person in our life? We should like to tell the Lord, as it were, that we are prepared to accept a double act: he and us; many a time us and him. But is that right?

Mary was not like that. She was submissive with a docility which permeated her mind and her desire to know and learn, but it permeated above all her will and her heart. That was how she came to be taken up with the things of the Lord and they became her concern through her acceptance and unconditional availability, through her tireless service.

And we can see that Mary by acting in this way left nothing out. Acting like this she offered to the Lord all the areas of her life for the Lord to fill. And the Lord did it.

What an example, what a call, what a road to perfection and salvation, taught us by this woman, the most faithful to the Lord, the most loving of Christ, the most devoted in her service.

And how much faith, how much renunciation and self-denial are necessary to become transparent to the light of the Lord, yielding to his grace, sensitive to his promptings, and most intimately alive above all to his grace and love.

The name of Mary

In the sixth month the angel Gabriel was sent by God to a town in Galilee called Nazareth, to a virgin engaged to a man whose name was Joseph, of the house of David. The virgin's name was Mary. And he came to her and said, "Greetings, favoured one! The Lord is with you." But she was much perplexed by his words and pondered what sort of greeting this might be. The angel said to her, "Do not be afraid, Mary, for you have found favour with God. And now, you will conceive in your womb and bear a son, and you will name him Jesus. He will be great, and will be called the Son of the Most High, and the Lord God will give to him the throne of his ancestor David. He will reign over the house of Jacob for ever, and of his kingdom there will be no end."

Mary said to the angel, "How can this be, since I have no husband?" The angel said, "The Holy Spirit will come upon you and the power of the Most High will overshadow you; therefore the child to be born will be holy; he will be called Son of God. And now, your relative Elizabeth in her old age has also conceived a son; and this is the sixth month for her who was said to be barren. For nothing will be impossible with God." Then Mary said, "Here am I, the servant of the Lord; let it be with me according to your word." Then the angel departed from her (Lk 1:26-38).

Luke's Gospel reminds us how the Virgin Mary entered into Christ's mystery. She entered it through the greeting of an angel and by making herself available to become the sanctuary of the Incarnation.

She received the Lord, and of all the times God has visited human beings there is no doubt that this is the most mysterious, the most wonderful, the one which most gives him glory. He came to visit his servant-girl. And his servant received him with her silent adoring faith, and with her body became God's sanctuary and tabernacle.

And acceptance also became her way of giving: she gave herself to the Lord, allowed herself to be taken and possessed, and thus was completed in her the wonderful exchange of God's love. God filled Mary and Mary clothed the Word of God in flesh: 'the mysterious exchange' which was the origin of the Incarnation involving us all and every one, you and me alike.

This mother's name is Mary. And thereby that name is a glorious one, glorious because of God and glorious because of this woman, tabernacle of the Most High.

We too glorify it, magnify its glory, contemplate its holiness. But let us allow her name and her life to inspire our life.

We have been meditating on Jesus' visit to Martha and Mary. But this Mary far surpasses the other because she welcomed him, believed him, listened to him, watched over him, fed the Word of God, making the Word her food. What a marvel! What splendour of omnipotence, glory, magnificence. But what a vocation, what a task, what a responsibility on Mary's part to remain faithful!

The greatness of her faith in believing that God had done such great things, in accepting a mission to motherhood unheard of, unutterable, not only by reason of her virginity which ran counter to it but also by reason of the divinity which enfolded it!

But the lowly handmaiden believed.

She did not understand, because God's mysteries remain mysterious, and the greater they are the more true this is. But she believed.

She believed in silent adoration, in silent obedience, in faithful persevering service.

This is Mary, this is our sister instructing us. But this also is our mother helping us to imitate her so that the Lord may find a welcome, so that the Word of God incarnate may find in our life that adoring active openness that he wants, for his glory and our salvation.